The Key to Florida

REG BUTLER

In Association with

THOMSON HOLIDAYS

1993

SETTLE PRESS

While every reasonable care has been taken by the author and publisher in presenting the information in this book, no responsibility can be taken by them or by Thomson Holidays for any inaccuracies. Information and prices were correct at time of printing.

First published by Settle Press
10 Boyne Terrace Mews
London W11 3LR

ISBN (Paperback) 1 872876 08 0

Printed by Villiers Publications Ltd
26a Shepherds Hill, London N6 5AH
Cover by Thumb Design Partnership
Cover photo from Florida Dept. of Commerce
Maps by Mary Butler

Foreword

As Britain's leading holiday company operating to Florida, Thomson are happy to be associated with Reg Butler's newly revised book 'The Key to Florida'.

You may be planning an independent style holiday with a self-drive car and a flexible itinerary. Or you may have booked a one- or two-centre holiday with all accommodation already arranged. Whatever your planning, we feel this pocket guide-book can be helpful in outlining Florida's enormous potential – beaches, sightseeing, theme parks and other attractions.

It's impossible to see everything in two weeks. When the holiday is over, we suggest you keep this guide-book to help plan your return visit.

Finally, all prices mentioned in the text were accurate at the time of printing. But remember there's also a 6.5% Sales Tax; and USA, too, has an inflation problem, though it's relatively modest. However, the quoted prices can serve as guidance to the average level of expenses.

THOMSON HOLIDAYS 1993

Contents

Maps

Chapter One

Florida – a State of Leisure

The biggest surprise for most first-time visitors to Florida is the enormous variety of things to see and do. Walt Disney World® Resort is the magnet which draws millions of visitors to Orlando. But around that nucleus in Central Florida there are dozens more theme parks and attractions that cover every possible interest.

Within one or two hours' drive there are superb sandy beaches, equipped with every imaginable aid to watersport. The entire coast of Florida is fringed with 'barrier islands' that offer choice of over a thousand miles of beaches, secluded or sophisticated, whichever you prefer.

The inevitable comparison, and competition, is with the Mediterranean. But Florida has several trump cards which help make a holiday even better than expected. There's the huge benefit of no language barrier. The quality and value of the food is first-class. The standard of service is excellent, and always given with a friendly smile.

Florida is a world class holiday destination. Blessed with a superb climate, the Sunshine State has a head start in the travel business. Catering for more than 40 million visitors every year, tourism is Florida's largest industry. Orlando Airport has matured into the 25th busiest airport in the world.

Florida is a big area – about the size of England and Wales combined, with a population of around 12 million. When you're staying in Orlando, you can't do the Florida Keys in a day!

Most first-time visitors start with maybe a week in Orlando for the fantasy of the Theme Parks with time to relax, and then the remainder of their holiday in the other world of beaches, alligators, birdlife, golf or watersport.

Walt Disney World Resort must certainly rate as the greatest entertainment complex on earth. It includes three mammoth theme parks, each being far bigger and crammed with highly professional showmanship than anything in Europe. Each of these parks takes a complete day to explore.

In addition there's the world's largest water-theme park, the 56-acre Typhoon Lagoon; and also an 11-acre

Discovery Island with still more water features. It takes four full days to skim the surface of Walt Disney World – and there'll still be many odd corners left unseen, ready for your next visit.

The Magic Kingdom® Park alone is 108 acres in extent, packed with brilliant entertainment. It's a complete dream-world for children, and an exercise in nostalgia for adults. But that's merely one small corner of the 28,000-acre site, of which 5,000 acres have been developed since 1981, including three championship-grade golf courses. Still more expansion is planned, into the 21st century.

Another corner of the Disney empire is the separate EPCOT Center®. Half of EPCOT Center is devoted to Future Worlds – dazzling displays of energy, transport, land, sea and imagination. It conveys all the excitement and fascination of life on earth. In EPCOT's World Showcase, over a dozen nations display their charms around a lagoon, so that you can walk from UK to China by way of Morocco.

In the Disney-MGM Studios® Theme Park you can learn the secrets of movie making, with tours of the production facilities. Among the numerous attractions, you can experience a flood or an earthquake, get drowned, or crushed by 20-ton rocks. It's lots of fun.

Close to the Disney complex, the rival Universal Studios have King Kong to greet millions of people to a Florida version of the film-studio attraction which has proved so popular in California.

In fact, both Disney-MGM and Universal are operating complete movie and TV sound stages, setting Orlando on course to become the largest film production centre outside Hollywood.

Even beyond these huge developments, there are still more theme parks and themed banquet attractions, spread like satellites within a short drive of Walt Disney World and Universal.

Sea World of Florida, for instance, offers scope for another day completely filled with show productions of killer whales, dolphins, sea lions and seals; waterski and speed boat shows; alligators, penguins and sharks. Don't miss it!

There are also plenty of opportunities to make a splash yourself. Quite apart from Walt Disney World's water theme parks, there's choice of Water Mania or Wet 'n Wild, which both offer every kind of water-slide excitement.

A short drive further south and there's the more tranquil attraction of Cypress Gardens – a flower-lover's paradise which also rates as Florida's first-ever theme park, dating back to the 'thirties. The daily shows include water-skiing, high diving and ice skating.

Entrance fees to the big-time Theme Parks are totally inclusive of all the shows, sights and rides. Florida is also

GEORGIA
to Tallahassee
to Panama City & Pensacola
Jacksonville
ATLANTIC OCEAN
St. Augustine
Ocala
Daytona Beach
Cape Canaveral
Orlando
Kissimmee
Cocoa Beach
Melbourne
Clearwater
Tampa
St. Petersburg
Sarasota
Fort Pierce
Lake Okeechobee
GULF OF MEXICO
Fort Myers
Sanibel-Captiva
Palm Beach
Fort Lauderdale
Naples
Miami
The Everglades
FLORIDA
Flamingo
Key Largo
Key West

packed with free, or nearly-free parks, attractions, tours and sights. Thanks to the excellent roads, tailor-made for relaxed driving, extremely wide choice comes within easy range of a self-drive car, wherever you're staying. The state still has wide open space to enjoy the best free amenity of all – mile after mile of unspoilt natural beauty. And it costs nothing to sit on a beach.

One of Florida's greatest attractions is the Kennedy Space Center, only one hour from Orlando. Admission is free, but you pay $7 ($4 for children) for well-organised bus tours of the immense Cape Canaveral site. Halts are made for demonstrations where moon astronauts were trained, and you drive close to the massive launch pad installations.

Possibly the most memorable sight is the Apollo spacecraft exhibit, with a 364-ft rocket laid on its side and dissected into its component modules.

When the heat's on, it doesn't cost much to cool off in one of Florida's 27 major crystal clear springs. Swim, take a boat ride or float with an inner-tube in refreshing waters for economical summertime enjoyment. Many of the springs are located within state parks and have standard entrance fees from $1 to $2.

Man-made attractions get most of the commercial publicity, but Florida's natural features can delight the dedicated nature-lover.

Consider, for instance, an out-of-this-world visit to Sanibel Island where gorgeous beaches are kept sparkling by the tidal waters of the Gulf of Mexico. If you're in a hurry, you don't belong in this palm-tree paradise. This is where Indians lived for a few thousand years, dining off seafood and piling millions of discarded shells to form hillocks that still remain among the mangroves.

Rent a bike and potter around miles of bicycle paths, enjoying this former Indian territory. There are lagoons and mangrove swamps, with rich birdlife everywhere: ospreys, heron, egrets, White Ibis, Roseate Spoonbill, Turkey Vultures. You'll really kick yourself if you don't take binoculars.

In the superb 'Ding' Darling wildlife sanctuary, it's easy to find alligators, dozing in the sun. Cost of entry is one dollar for pedestrians or cyclists, three dollars for a car – payable on an honour system of posting your contribution in a pillar-box. All the 450 wildlife refuges in USA follow this system, at the same price.

Florida can boast of more than a hundred state parks and reserves. Grand-daddy of them all is the Everglades National Park, which must rate high among the best-known in the world. There you can see first-hand the wild and primitive setting which was experienced by the early pioneers.

Beaches aren't the only places you can enjoy Florida on a budget. Many attractions and festivals, scattered all over the state, are free. The year-round calendar is full of cultural, historical and recreational activities for the entire family. Check on arrival to find "What's On".

At a very reasonable cost, you can also tour great art galleries, museums and semi-tropical gardens. Florida is well stocked with all the great masters of classical painting, through to the world's largest collection of Salvador Dali's work outside of Spain.

By European standards, America may seem young and brash. But Americans themselves, touring their own USA, are keenly interested in making the most of their few centuries of history.

Even though Florida was about the first area of USA to be explored, with establishment of a few scattered 16th-century settlements, historic remains are in short supply compared with Europe.

Anywhere you go, buildings still standing from the 19th century are cherished as historic museumpieces, filled with relics of the pioneer past, and heavily promoted to attract tourists – that is, mainly American tourists. But there's no reason why a British visitor can't get just as much enjoyment, gazing in awe at anything that's a hundred years old.

There's even a Florida version of Britain's Stately Homes circuit. In late 19th century and early 20th, America's wealthiest tycoons were lured by Florida's climate to build winter homes. Several are open to visitors, such as railwayman Henry Flagler's mansion in Palm Beach, Rockefeller's two-storey home at Ormond Beach, circus-magnate Ringling's Venetian-style palace at Sarasota, Edison's winter retreat at Fort Myers, or International Harvester's John Deering at Villa Vizcaya, on Biscayne Bay, Miami.

On a less palatial scale you can visit house museums associated with the likes of Ernest Hemingway, Audubon the naturalist, or US President Harry Truman. You'll find all three in Key West.

Florida is a great place for the sports-lover, whether it's spectator or do-it-yourself. The climate is idyllic for watersports. Waterskiing, windsurfing and sailing prevail on the Gulf Coast and inland on the lakes. Boating, waterskiing, surfing and body surfing flourish along the Atlantic shores. Inland, water theme parks offer highly imaginative facilities for keeping wet and cool. Scuba-diving and snorkelling is fantastic along the Florida Keys.

Every resort, however small, can offer a good choice of golf courses, tennis courts and riding stables. In many locations there are opportunities to watch first-hand some of those all-American sports like baseball, football and basketball, besides the Hispanic import of jai-alai.

You can capture many different flavours in Florida: a taste of Cuba or Haiti in Miami; a Caribbean conch republic along the Florida Keys; memories of Greece in

Tarpon Springs; Scotland in Dunedin; Venice along the canals of Fort Lauderdale; the grace of the Old South in Florida's Panhandle that borders Alabama and Georgia; or back to the primitive in the Everglades.

Two things stand out about Florida.

Firstly, there's the remarkable range of things to do, places to visit, and the incredible variety of the theme parks.

Secondly, once you've paid the cost of trans-Atlantic travel, all the expenses on accommodation, food, self-drive transport and general etceteras total up less than you'd pay in Britain or continental Europe. Where else can you find a large and comfortable room for a family of four, for £30? Or petrol under £1 a gallon? Or a good 3-course meal for a fiver?

That combination of value-for-money and catering for every taste is what makes the Florida travel industry tick. On the homeward flight, most holidaymakers are thinking about where to go in Florida "next time". You can't see it all in two weeks!

Chapter Two

Choosing a Holiday

The prime destination is Orlando and its wealth of theme parks and other man-made and natural attractions. But the diversity of Florida makes it an ideal two-centre destination – to combine time at Orlando with a contrasting beach-resort week, or to go touring with a self-drive car.

Which season to go?

In the Sunshine State, weather men never say it will be "partly cloudy". Instead, it's "mostly sunny". Florida is in the sunshine business, with peak demand from American clientele – 'snowbirds' – coming down from northern states, Christmas till April.

But possibly the better months for Florida are September till December; or May and June. There are fewer crowds; hotels and theme parks offer discounts; it's closer to British ideas of nice weather.

The high summer months are humid, with temperature into the 90's. Normally it then rains between 2 and 4 every afternoon, cooling things down. It's Nature's style of air conditioning, very welcome. On the Gulf coast, a one o'clock beach breeze rolls in with the surf to refresh the languid summer afternoons.

For budget-watchers, it's worth picking low season, which varies according to region. As a general rule, south and central Florida's low season rates operate in May and June, and September to December. North Florida's low season goes from November through March.

Incidentally, winter months are best for bird-spotting, when migrants from cooler regions fly down for the season.

Gateway to the beaches

Sitting in its Central Florida location, Orlando is the prime gateway to the east and west coast beaches.

An hour to the east are lively Daytona Beach, and very quiet beaches like New Smyrna, Cocoa and Melbourne, coupled with all the fascination of the Space Coast.

About two hours west are St. Petersburg and Clearwater Beach – family favourite Gulf resorts of the Pinellas Sun Coast – backed by the city attractions of Tampa.

Within three hours or so, southeast, are the Gold Coast beaches that centre on Fort Lauderdale, from Palm Beach to Miami, with plentiful night-time action and proximity to the Everglades.

Beaches are open and accessible year-round, with average annual sea temperature of 71 degrees. Surrounded by the warm, calm waters of the Gulf of Mexico on the west, and the stronger waves of the Atlantic on the east, Florida is blessed with a beach for every taste.

From the silvery beaches of the State's Northeast and mid-Atlantic coast to the shelling meccas of Sanibel and Captiva Islands, Florida offers 1,100 miles of shoreline.

Swimming, sunbathing, snorkelling, fishing and windsurfing are the top priorities, with time off for nature parks and sightseeing.

Pick your favourite colour – white, buff, orange or red – and then decide if you want to sunbathe on soft quartz sand, drive on hard-packed sand, walk on beaches of powdered seashells, or just enjoy the luxury of doing absolutely nothing at all.

Look closely at the map of Florida. Virtually the entire mainland is sheltered by long, thin "barrier islands". That's the standard sequence: the ocean, a sandy beach, a thin island only just above sea level, then a calm and relatively narrow lagoon crossed by an occasional bridge or causeway, and finally the mainland shore. Perfect for every choice of boating, cruising and water-sport! Only three resorts have their beaches on the mainland: Venice, Naples, and Mexico Beach near Panama City, all on the Gulf Coast.

Sport

Sport facilities are abundant. More than 900 golf courses and a myriad of tennis facilities are open daily at specialty resorts, local clubs, and municipal recreational parks throughout Florida. Typical green fees on a public course are $25 a round; $8 a day for tennis.

Fishing? Saltwater fish, like grouper, snapper and tarpon to name just a few, are available all along the 1,100-mile coastline. Bass, carp and other freshwater fish inhabit Florida's 30,000 lakes. Almost 200 rivers provide additional opportunities for fishing, canoeing and swimming.

Spectator sports? The competitive choice includes boat-racing, baseball, basketball, auto-racing, American-style football, golf, greyhound racing, horseracing, jai-alai, tennis and sailing regattas. Any time of year there's something happening. Check the local 'What's On' listings.

From mid-February to early April, 18 major American

baseball teams hold spring training in varied locations around Florida, with a programme of exhibition games that can cost $3.50 to $12. From April till September, the Orlando SunRays play professional baseball, with tickets costing $1.50 to $3.50.

Tickets for basketball start at around $4 or $6, depending on the stadium. Miami is home town of the Orange Bowl football game, with action from August to January.

Most major resorts have a Jai-Alai Fronton, with games several times weekly. Entrance fees are very modest, $1 to $5. Entrances to dog and horse racing events are likewise very low – profits come from the betting!

On the trail through Florida

Nature-lovers can explore lagoons, rivers and swamps on foot or afloat, amid landscapes that teem with several hundred species of birdlife. Sometimes you're only a few feet away from an alligator.

Go wandering through dense underbush with the fresh scent of pine in the air. Slush along the edge of a marshland watching a myriad egrets, woodstorks and Everglades kites. Canoe through black murky waters shielded from the light by banks of cypress and Spanish moss. Go horseback riding across the sands, or across open country. Try biking on old roadways and along well-planned paths to discover new vistas around every bend. The pancake-flat terrain is designed for Sunday riders on fat-tyred three-speeds.

These images of relaxation and discovery can all be experienced along the trails of Florida. With a land area of 54,252 square miles and 4,308 square miles of water, Florida has plenty of open space for hiking, biking and canoeing.

Fifty percent of the land area is wooded, providing shelter and food for an abundance of wildlife, including fox, coyotes and deer. More than 70 bird types can be seen at varying times of the year. Nearly half of the tree species native to USA can be found in Florida.

For canoeing, Florida is home to three basic river types: alluvial, blackwater and springfed. Alluvial rivers are brown-stained (or green) in colour, and carry sediments along with them; blackwater rivers are named for their deep colour caused by tannins from the swamp and pine forests; and springfed rivers are usually very clear.

Recreational trails can be found throughout the State. Three national forests and the Everglades National Park have their own trail system. The "Ding" Darling National Wildlife Refuge on Sanibel Island features canoe trails and a five-mile scenic drive. Most of Florida's 100-odd state parks offer their own nature trails suitable for hiking, biking and canoeing. Wherever you go, it's easy to rent bikes, canoes and boats.

Take a Cruise

Whether venturing out of Miami, Tampa, Fort Lauderdale, Palm Beach, Port Canaveral, Fort Myers or Jacksonville, a cruise can be part of the Florida experience. Around 30 cruise lines serve Florida, offering a variety of formats and destinations.

Pre-booked, there are week-long Caribbean cruises, and 3-day or 4-day packages to the Bahamas. You can even do a one-day round trip to the Bahamas; or just sail up and down offshore for an excuse to gamble afloat (casinos are illegal in Florida).

For another change of pace, you can spend an afternoon or evening floating along rivers or the Intracoastal Waterway. Some prefer a daytime excursion, while others choose a romantic evening under the stars.

Go sightseeing

Nature is not the only beauty that Florida has to offer. Some of her smaller towns have unique styles of architecture, brilliant gardens and historical landmarks. Local chambers of commerce or visitor's centres often give out information leaflets about self-guided walking and biking tours along "urban trails".

Among the best-known town trails are Miami's Art Deco District; St. Augustine's restored Spanish Quarter; Winter Park, north of Orlando; Ybor Square in Tampa; and downtown Key West.

For the scenic minded, Florida beckons from highway billboards, reminding you of attractions just along the road: from man-made theme parks and historic sites to recreation areas and state parks.

For the history buff there are ruins of old forts and restored plantations, ancient 19th-century cobbled streets, and specialty museums galore. On the cultural circuit, there's a wide range of art galleries and museums.

Just 'pick and mix' for a holiday packed with variety!

Self-drive car

Though public transportation is available, the economy of renting a car in Florida, the freedom it affords, and the ease of travel on Florida's super-highways and interstate system, make car rental a most attractive option. Without wheels amid the broad boulevards and avenues you are nowhere. The pedestrian is an extinct species, apart from joggers.

To see Florida, reckon a self-drive car as *essential*. With two or more in your party, it's easily the most economical option. The first time you fill up, it's hard to believe how little it costs.

Driving is relaxed, with a 55 mph speed limit along most of the superb highways, and some stretches where 65 mph is allowed. As a reminder, signs proclaim "Florida enforces the law - Drive 55". It makes for non-competitive driving, laid-back and courteous. Out-of-town traffic density is low compared with the width of the highways. You can safely admire the scenery and still make good mileage.

The road view of Florida shows the immensity of those wide open spaces. Even though it's flat everywhere, there are many scenic drives, especially if you keep off the boring turnpikes.

Finding accommodation

Priced to fit every budget, lodging around Florida offers widest possible choice – from bed and breakfast inns to luxury resort complexes that feature everything from water-ski lessons to horseback riding.

Roadside motels plead for your custom: "Spend a night, not a fortune." Normally the motels don't coyly hide their room rate behind a wardrobe door, but blazon it so you can see "how much" from a hundred yards away. Motorist cabins advertise ultra-low rates off-season: they'd rather have fewer dollars than empty rooms. These cabins often include simple self-catering facilities.

At coastal resorts, prices partly depend on how much ocean you can see from your bedroom window. Save money by renting a hotel or motel room a block or more from the beach. Most resorts are ribbon-developed, long and thin along the shoreline. So you can still be only a stone's throw away.

Generally, room rates compare favourably with Europe, at hotels and motels with surprisingly spacious rooms and good facilities. Rooms are usually big enough to permit children under 18 to stay free with parents, making Florida an ideal family travel destination. Senior citizens often get discounts on room rates.

All prices yo-yo up and down according to season. A well-publicized festival or ball game will send tariffs rocketing for hard-to-find accommodation. Maybe the following week the rates will plunge again, as the 'Vacancies' signs are switched on.

For go-as-you-please hotel accommodation, a popular idea is to buy prepaid vouchers featuring room-only deals at famous hotel chains. Each voucher normally covers a large room sleeping up to four persons in two king-sized double beds. Accommodation can be reserved by "toll free" telephone.

How many miles from Orlando?

Cape Canaveral 46; Clearwater 74; Daytona Beach 54; Fort Lauderdale 205; Fort Myers 153; Fort Walton Beach 359; Jacksonville 133; Key West 371; Kissimmee 6; Miami 232; Ocala 72; Panama City 334; Pensacola 435; Sarasota 132; St. Augustine 61; St. Petersburg 66; Tallahassee 242; Tampa 85; West Palm Beach 166.

Personal recommendations

Bird watchers – Sanibel
Cigar smokers – Tampa
Clowns – Venice
Conchologists – Sanibel
Croquet and polo players – Palm Beach
Culture vultures – Sarasota
Families – Orlando, Orlando, and any beach
Film-goers – Universal and MGM Studios, Orlando
Gardeners – Orlando for Cypress and other Gardens
Gays – Key West
Golfers – just about anywhere
Hell's Angels – Daytona Beach
Hemingway fans – Key West
Historians – St. Augustine
Inventors – Fort Myers
Millionaires – Palm Beach
Mountaineers – take the next flight out
Scuba-divers – Key Largo
Spanish linguists – Miami
Speedway supporters – Daytona Beach
Spongers – Tarpon Springs
Student Spring-breakers – Fort Lauderdale; Daytona Beach
Surfers – east coast from Daytona Beach to Sebastian Inlet, but not Gulf Coast
Wind-surfers – best on Gulf Coast

Monthly Weather Statistics:

ORLANDO:

	J	F	M	A	M	J	J	A	S	O	N	D
MAX	71	72	76	82	87	89	90	90	88	83	76	72
MIN	50	51	56	61	66	71	73	74	72	66	57	52
RAIN	2.3	3.0	3.5	2.7	2.9	7.1	8.3	6.7	7.7	4.1	1.6	1.9

TAMPA:

	J	F	M	A	M	J	J	A	S	O	N	D
MAX	71	72	76	82	88	90	90	90	89	84	72	72
MIN	50	52	56	62	67	72	74	74	73	66	56	51
RAIN	2.3	2.9	3.9	2.1	2.4	6.5	8.4	8.0	6.4	2.5	1.8	2.2

MIAMI:

	J	F	M	A	M	J	J	A	S	O	N	D
MAX	76	77	80	83	85	88	89	90	88	85	80	77
MIN	59	59	63	67	71	74	76	76	75	71	65	60
RAIN	2.2	2.0	2.1	3.6	6.1	9.0	6.9	6.7	8.7	8.2	2.7	1.6

SEA TEMPERATURES

	72	74	75	77	82	86	88	90	86	82	77	74

Chapter Three

Orlando – gateway to Florida

Some claim that Florida's 1200 miles of coastline are the state's greatest asset. Yet Central Florida, with not one inch of coastline, has become one of the world's greatest tourist destinations. It has almost 80,000 hotel guest rooms (second in number only to Las Vegas); 4,500 restaurants; an international airport with an average 450 scheduled flights per day; and some of the world's best known family attractions and outdoor recreation opportunities.

As you fly in to Orlando, the first impression is how green Florida looks from the air, with thick woodlands, and water everywhere to irrigate lush lawns and golf courses.

On arrival at the airport, you pass through the usual procedures: Immigration, Customs and Agriculture. About the toughest questioning is at the Agriculture desk, where any fresh fruit, eggs, sandwiches or yoghurt will be confiscated.

Out of the airport, downtown Orlando and Winter Park lie a few miles north, up State Road 436 or 527 – Orange Avenue.

Due west on State Road 482 takes you to the International Drive area, where numerous hotels, restaurants and varied attractions are located.

Southwest along Interstate 4 leads to Walt Disney World, with numerous other big attractions spaced along the highways towards Kissimmee. Reckon a 20-mile drive from Orlando to Walt Disney World.

Transport

You'll soon appreciate why a self-drive car is essential. Local bus lines offer a shuttle coach service from selected hotels in Orlando and Kissimmee to Walt Disney World and Sea World, while some hotels operate their own shuttle service. But there are other locations you'll want to visit, and – because of the distances involved – taxis come very pricey.

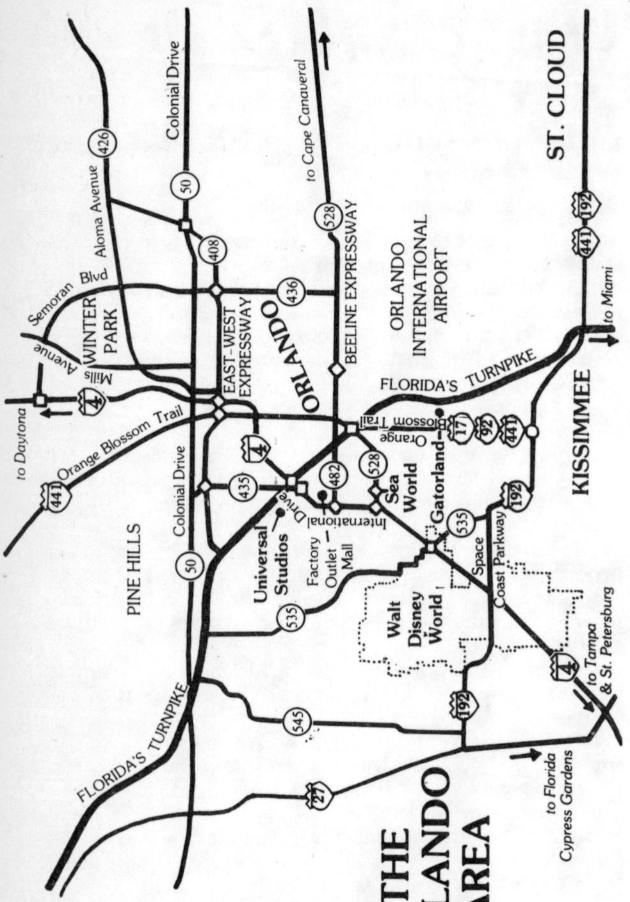

THE ORLANDO AREA

The big-time attractions

See chapter 4 for a summary of what's on offer at Walt Disney World; chapter 5 for other theme parks and daytime attractions; chapter 6 for nightlife suggestions.

What else besides Theme Parks?

Citrus farming, strawberry fields, and cattle raising are also predominant in Central Florida. It's interesting to see these activities first-hand. Cattle auctions are held every Wednesday at Kissimmee.

Ocala, north of Orlando, is Florida's horsebreeding area. World class thoroughbreds are raised amid green grassy hills, a rival to Kentucky. Visit a stud farm and, to the layman, every horse looks ready to go for the Derby.

In small centres, county fairs and agricultural festivals are scheduled through the year.

The area also features a full calendar of annual events based on sport or the performing arts. Typical fixtures include the Citrus Bowl, the Du Pont Tennis Classic, and a Shakespeare Festival in Orlando; the St. Cloud Art Festival; the Florida Blueberry Festival in Ocala; and the bi-annual Silver Spurs Rodeo in Kissimmee.

Winter Park

Founded as a winter resort in the late 1890's, Winter Park now occupies a special place in the heart of Greater Orlando. Its main street, Park Avenue, is filled with European-style shops, secluded garden patios, exclusive stores for men and women, antique and art galleries and restaurants that range from gourmet dining rooms to snack bars.

Highly recommended: take a boat trip costing about $5 – kids half price – for a one-hour tour through 12 miles of lakes and canals, past beautiful estates, manicured gardens and the background sound of the resident bird-life.

Sport facilities

Central Florida has around four dozen golf courses and 21 tennis centres with more than 800 courts. Among the prestigious tennis and golf resorts are Lake Nona, Grand Cypress and Grenelefe. When you tread the grass, it's like deep-pile carpeting. Energetic golfers clamber in and out of their electric golf carts as they aim for 27 or 36 holes in a day. Green fees vary widely, but check at your hotel for any special deals they have negotiated. Incidentally, alligators eat golf-balls. Hit your ball off the fairway, and an alligator may get there first.

Hot air over Orlando

For the thrill-of-a-lifetime, consider a hot-air balloon trip over Orlando. Local companies offer balloon flights which normally start early morning when the air is calm, with only a light breeze.

It takes about 20 minutes to set up the balloon, ready for take-off. Then about 45 minutes to an hour for the ride, the pilot keeping in radio contact with the chase crew. A skilled pilot can give you the bonus excitement of doing a 'Splash and Dash' in the lake. The aim is just to skim the water surface to create ripples. Get it wrong, and it becomes 'Swamp and Swim'! Then finally there's a few minutes of tree-topping – brushing the bottom of the basket with the top wispy branches of the trees – and a landing in scrubland.

Typical cost is $250 per couple, insurance included.

Go boating

Hundreds of lakes and rivers offer numerous water sports including canoeing, powerboating, tubing, waterskiing, sailing, fishing – especially for bass – and swimming.

In more sedentary fashion, it's worth sampling the choice of guided boat trips, especially along the narrow creeks and peaceful swamp areas where Seminole Indians formerly paddled in dug-outs. In fact, why not rent a silent canoe for $5 an hour? Try Shingle Creek, at Kissimmee, for instance.

There are so many rewarding sights. Large and beautiful butterflies flutter against a background of Spanish moss hanging from cypress trees. Along the bank, turtles with yellow waistcoats watch the passing boats. During the June–September period there's a good chance of spotting alligator, enjoying a sleepy-eyed siesta in the sun.

Spectator sports

Among the many tournaments scheduled each year are the DuPont Tennis Classic, the Nestle Invitational at Bay Hill, the Grand Cypress Golf Tournament and the Walt Disney World Golf Tournament.

Orlando Arena, a 15,000 seat facility located in the downtown Centroplex, is home to the city's new National Basketball Association team, the Orlando Magic. The Arena also schedules concerts, ice shows, rodeos and other special events.

West of downtown Orlando is the 70,000-capacity **Florida Citrus Bowl**, home to the annual Florida Citrus Bowl played in January. Other sporting events, concerts and exhibitions are held here.

Regular meetings are held for horse and greyhound racing and the Spanish sport of Jai-Alai. Entrance fees are just a dollar or two; the profits come from Tote-style gambling called pari-mutuel.

Shopping

The Orlando area offers a full range of American-style shopping. There are traditional malls such as Altamonte Fashion Square, Florida, and Colonial Plaza; and shopping villages – Church Street Exchange, Church Street Market, Crossroads, Mercado Mediterranean Shopping Village, the Marketplace, Old Towne and Walt Disney World Village.

Park Avenue in Winter Park blends old and new with specialty stores and exclusive boutiques. Factory stores such as Belz Factory Outlet and Quality Outlet offer factory-gate prices. Flea World in Sanford is open Friday till Sunday, and has an unusual mixture of merchandise ranging from fresh produce to imported clothing.

(See also chapter 15 for more shopping information.)

Chapter Four

The World of Walt Disney

Walt Disney World is home to the Magic Kingdom, Epcot Center and the Disney-MGM Studios Theme Park. Along with two water parks, a nightclub theme park, 10 themed resorts, 99 holes of golf, dinner shows, horseback riding, water recreation and white-sand beaches, it's a complete world of escapism. The range of Walt Disney World options is far wider than just for 'a family day out'. Adult visitors outnumber children three to one.

Occupying a 43-square-mile site, Walt Disney World Resort opened in 1971. Around ten square miles have been developed, while another eleven square miles are designated as a wilderness preserve. Development continues, with new projects in the pipeline. It's all part of an ambitious 10-year expansion which the parent company calls the Disney Decade.

One point stands out. There's no way that anyone can nip round Walt Disney World in a day. Each of the Theme Parks needs at least a full day to get your money's-worth. A popular purchase is the Four-Day World Passport – needn't be consecutive days. On a one-week stay in Orlando, many people alternate between Disney and trips elsewhere; or they visit other major attractions in the area.

Operating as a show-business kingdom with a cast – *not* employees – of 32,000, there is enormous attention to detail. Every scrap of litter is instantly removed. Everybody smiles. All of Walt Disney World's a stage. "Have a nice day!"

Location

Walt Disney World Resort is located 20 miles southwest of Orlando along Interstate 4 with exits for the Walt Disney World Village, Epcot Center and (via U.S. 192) the Magic Kingdom and Disney-MGM Studios Theme Park.

Epcot Center is three miles south of Magic Kingdom (two miles west of Walt Disney World Village and a mile northeast of the Disney-MGM Studios Theme Park) and is linked by monorail to the Magic Kingdom and surface transit to other guest areas.

The Magic Kingdom and the Epcot Center each have parking for more than 12,000 vehicles. Take very careful note of where you park your car, or you won't find it till midnight!

Opening times, and tickets

The Magic Kingdom, the Epcot Center, and the Disney/MGM Studios Theme Park open year-round at 9 a.m. every day. During most of the year, the Magic Kingdom stays open till 7 p.m., Epcot Center till 8 p.m., and Disney/MGM Studios till 7 p.m. The closing hours fluctuate according to season. Extended hours – sometimes up to 11 p.m. or midnight – are set for peak vacation times, typically when most American children are on summer holiday, and at Thanksgiving, Christmas and Easter.

One-day tickets are sold for Magic Kingdom, Epcot Center, or Disney MGM Studios Theme Park individually. Best Buy for most visitors is the Three Parks Passport which includes admission on any four days, unlimited use of attractions at all parks, and monorail, ferryboat or bus transportation between the resort areas.

Magic Kingdom

Based on the design of Disneyland in California, the Magic Kingdom covers 100 acres and offers 45 major shows and adventures in seven 'lands': Main Street, U.S.A.; Adventureland; Frontierland; Liberty Square; Fantasyland; Tomorrowland, and Mickey's Starland.

The many popular attractions include Mickey Mouse's house in Starland plus Pirates of the Caribbean, Big Thunder Mountain Railroad, Haunted Mansion and Space Mountain. Dreamflight in Tomorrowland is a voyage of discovery into the past and future of air travel.

In Main Street USA, there is music everywhere. Barbershoppers harmonize on street corners, and there is old-time strumming on banjoes. You are lured to Adventureland, where the greatest danger en route is of being run over by a horse tram.

Now and then you may meet famed movie stars like Mickey Mouse, Donald Duck and Pluto. Just watch the little kids! When they meet Mickey and maybe shake hands, it's an experience like meeting the Pope, their faces alight with awe and wonder.

Feeling hungry? You can lunch off freshly battered shrimps, popcorn, footlong hotdogs or gourmet Hamburgers. Other dining choices abound. There are more than 3,000 distinct menu items served at food locations in Walt Disney World. Dodge the one o'clock line-ups! Early-day reservations can mean the best selection of meal-times and menu options. Magic Kingdom is an alcohol-free zone, but they do a neat line in iced tea.

Epcot Center

The Experimental Prototype Community of Tomorrow (EPCOT) is a 260-acre exposition which splits into two main areas: World Showcase pavilions that highlight eleven countries; and Future World, in which nine corporate pavilions examine past and future technology.

Future World uses highly imaginative technology to focus on discovery and scientific achievements. Major attractions, and their sponsors, are:
Spaceship Earth (AT&T), Universe of Energy (EXXON), World of Motion (General Motors), Journey into Imagination (Eastman Kodak), The Land (Kraft), Computer General (Unisys), Horizons (General Electric), The Living Seas (United Technologies Corp.), and Wonders of Life (Metropolitan Life).

Wonders of Life is the newest of Future World's nine major attractions. The Wonders of Life pavilion is a sometimes whimsical, sometimes serious, presentation which includes a thrill ride through the human body.

World Showcase presents the culture, entertainment, crafts and architecture of nations worldwide. You can go around the world in a day, saving enormously on fares, visiting Canada, UK, France, Morocco, Japan, Italy, Germany, China, Mexico, Norway and USA. All of them feature restaurants that offer their national cuisine.

Disney-MGM Studios Theme Park

This 135-acre attraction located south of Epcot Center includes a working motion-picture and television studio, a themed entertainment park, and a guided tour of production facilities.

When the attraction opened in 1989, public response was so overwhelming that Disney announced plans to double its size over the next few years.

Lights, cameras and all the action of Hollywood film making are "on stage" for visitors to the combination movie and TV production facility. Shows and attractions are based on elements of showbiz, while a Backstage Studio Tour takes visitors into the land of backlots, special-effects areas and sound stage.

Attractions include The Great Movie Ride, SuperStar Television and the Monster Sound Show, the Indiana Jones Epic Stunt Spectacular, and Star Tours (based on the space thriller 'Star Wars'). Among recent additions to the new park are Miss Piggy and Kermit the Frog, lead players in Muppet Vision 3-D.

Themed restaurants such as the 50s Prime Time Cafe, Hollywood-style shops and street entertainment add an extra layer to the Tinseltown theme.

Dodge the queues

Nobody wants to shuffle 50 minutes through a cattle-stall system, for a 10-minute ride. Follow these tips to minimize queuing time.

It sounds odd, but the busiest days in the Magic Kingdom and Epcot Center are Monday to Wednesday. At the Disney-MGM Theme Park, busiest days are Wednesday to Friday. Weekends are least busy, because that's when big numbers of holidaymakers to Orlando are arriving or departing.

Conclusion: if your travel plans can't fit a weekend visit, plan Disney-MGM Studios Theme Park earlier in the week, and do Epcot Center and Magic Kingdom later in the week.

Magic Kingdom strategy – Arrive early, like 8.30. Ignore everything on Main Street and leg it to Adventureland and do the Jungle Cruise and Pirates of the Caribbean before the queues build up. Nip through to Frontierland for Big Thunder Mountain. Try to re-schedule your stomach to accept a mid-morning snack, skip the noontime lunch queues, and take in more calories during mid-afternoon.

Epcot Center strategy – On arrival, go left! Walk past the queue for Spaceship Earth and head for Future World East (to the left). Arriving early, make Wonders of Life your first stop. Other Future World East attractions: Universe of Energy, Horizons, and World of Motion.

Alternate strategy: head for World Showcase (the "back" of the park) in the morning, saving Future World for later in the day.

"What time is the 3-o'clock parade?" Live entertainment in all three theme parks is ever-changing. Weekly show schedules are available at information locations: City Hall (Magic Kingdom), Earth Station (Epcot Center) and Guest Services Building (Disney-MGM Studios Theme Park).

Cool-it. Average daily high temperatures range from 70 F to 90+ F depending upon time of year. Cool, comfortable clothing and sunscreen are two ways to beat the heat. Two more ideas: Typhoon Lagoon and River Country water parks. During the season of extended hours, plan to arrive early. Then exit the theme parks during the noontime heat, and head for the cool waters. Remember to get a handstamp for later theme park re-entry.

Oh, my poor feet! EPCOT could stand for Every Person Comes Out Tired. The promenade around World Showcase Lagoon at Epcot Center is a favourite stroll, but it's 1.2 miles, and that's only a small portion of the wear-and-tear on your feet. Comfortable footwear is a must.

Other Disney World attractions

Typhoon Lagoon

Billed by Disney as the world's largest water-thrill park, the sophisticated 56-acre Typhoon Lagoon is four times the size of Disney's River Country (the granddaddy of water parks).

The centrepiece is a 95-foot mountain which must rank as the Everest of Central and Southern Florida. Brave people scale the mountain by stairs but cascade down on a choice of eight water slides and white-water tubing flumes.

A 2½-acre wave-making lagoon lies at the base of the mountain. Six-ft breakers bring the seashore to Central Florida, giving body surfers the chance to show off.

The park also includes the 362,000-gallon Shark Reef, in which snorkellers swim alongside fish, rays and other reef creatures, but curiously no sharks.

Castaway Creek is a meandering 700-yard rafting stream encircling the complex, and there's a special water-play area for the kids.

River Country and Discovery Island

Located in Fort Wilderness, River Country is an old-fashioned swimmin' hole with water slides, flumes, white water rapids, nature trails, heated swimming pool and white sand beaches.

Just across the channel in Bay Lake is 11-acre Discovery Island, a tropical paradise of flowers and trails that feature birds and animals including sand cranes, brown pelicans and Galapagos turtles. But vultures have been moved off.

Other sport facilities include three championship golf courses; a 6-hole Executive Course; tennis courts; pools and lakes for swimming, boating, water skiing and fishing; jogging paths; and horseback riding.

Breakfast and Dinner Shows

Chip and Dale's Country Morning Jamboree – A Disney character breakfast at Ft. Wilderness Campground. Shows at 8 and 9.15 a.m. daily. 407/824-2803.

Broadway at the Top – Features popular show tunes, at Top of the World, Contemporary Resort Hotel. Shows at 6 and 9.15 p.m. daily. 407/824-3611.

Hoop-Dee-Doo Revue – Pioneer Hall, Ft. Wilderness Campground
A country and western vaudeville show with Disney characters. Shows at 5, 7.30 and 10 p.m. daily. 407/824-2803.

Polynesian Luau – Luau Cove, Polynesian Resort
A South Seas luau is a Hawaiian banquet with native entertainment and ritual dances. Shows at 6.45 p.m. and 9.30 p.m. daily. 407/824-1335.

Mickey's Tropical Revue – Luau Cove, Polynesian Resort
A South Seas luau with Mickey and Minnie and other Disney characters. Shows at 4.30 p.m. daily. 407/824-1335.

Pleasure Island – Adjacent to the Walt Disney World Marketplace, a nighttime entertainment complex with choice of discos, nightclubs, a 'Rocker RollerDome' and the Comedy Warehouse. Under-18's must be accompanied by a parent or guardian.

Chapter Five

Orlando - attractions galore

Quite apart from Walt Disney World, the Orlando and Kissimmee area of Central Florida offers several major competing Theme Parks, and numerous other attractions. There's never enough time to work through all the tempting ideas, especially if you also want to sample the Florida beaches. You can't go away without sampling a water park for a great range of slides, chutes, rafts and fountains. You might even go swimming.

Tourism statistics show that 90% of American holidaymakers in Florida are repeat visitors. Unless you're staying several weeks, it's only possible to skim the surface, and come back another year. Here's a short-list of what else is on offer besides Mickey Mouse.

Bok Tower Gardens – Lake Wales
A 128-acre sanctuary of gardens and nature trails, 15 minutes south of Cypress Gardens. Azaleas, camellias and magnolias provide seasonal displays of colour. Squirrels, quail and wood ducks roam the grounds. The Singing Tower, centred among pools and winding pathways, is a 255-foot stone and marble structure with 57 bronze bells which chime every half-hour. A 45-minute carillon recital is presented at 3 p.m. daily.
Open daily 8-17hrs. Adults $3; under-12's free. Tel: 813/676-1408.

Cypress Gardens – located 45 minutes southwest of Orlando off US 27 near Winter Haven.

More than half the park's 223 acres are devoted to floral settings, with over 8,000 varieties of plants and flowers among the towering cypress trees. Popular displays include 40-ft high bougainvillea, floss silk trees, bird of paradise and chrysanthemums. The All American Rose Garden includes 500 of USA's most popular rose varieties. An annual chrysanthemum festival takes place around mid-November. With more than two million blooms, it's the largest 'mums display in southeast USA. Southern Belles are happy to pose for pictures.

The gardens double as a wildlife haven. Visitors can

explore nature trails, an aviary and a forest that nurtures threatened and endangered wildlife.

Cypress Gardens also ranks as Florida's first theme park, established in the mid-'30s. Superb waterskiing shows are performed daily. "Everybody's Skiing Caribbean" includes slick barefooting stunts, ramp jumping, Delta Wing Kite stunts, swivel skiing and a spectacular four-tier human pyramid.

There are electric boat rides through a maze of canals. Kodak's Island in the Sky is a 153-ft high revolving platform that gives an overall aerial view.

USA's most elaborate model railway incorporates 1,100 feet of track, 400 buildings and 4,800 miniature human and animal figures. Cypress Junction re-creates typical American towns and scenery in all seasonal settings.

Open daily 9-18 hrs, with extended hours in peak seasons.
Adults $22.20, children $15.30. Tel: 813/324-2111

Sea World of Florida – 7007 Sea World Drive, Orlando
After Walt Disney World, this is central Florida's leading attraction, with over 4 million visitors a year. Sea World is located 10 minutes south of downtown Orlando, at the intersection of 1-4 and the Beeline Expressway. The park features Shamu, the killer whale, dolphins, sea lions and seals in a variety of themed show productions. "Terrors of the Deep" displays the world's largest collection of eels, sharks and poisonous and venomous fish in spectacular coral reef aquariums.

There is also a working brewery, a waterski and speed boat show, botanical gardens with alligators and exotic birds, a Hawaiian village, Penguin and Shark Encounters, Cap'n'Kids World, World of the Sea, and a Sky Tower ride.

Clyde and Seamore, stars of the sea lion and otter show, take you back to life in "10,000 B.C."

"Shamu: New Visions" gives viewers a vicarious thrill ride with Shamu through the use of underwater Sony cameras.

At the Atlantic Waterski Stadium, early American history comes to life in "Gold Rush Ski Show". In this action-packed melodrama, the Sea World skiers try to "strike it rich", while performing daring trick water skiing, long distance jumping, high speed barefooting and graceful water ski ballet. After dark entertainment includes a highly popular "Star Light Laser Spectacular".

Hint: get there early. Check the schedule of feeding times, and route yourself accordingly. There's an enormous amount to see, and you need all day to get round. For added interest, pay another $6 for a behind-the-scenes tour.
Open daily 9-19 hrs during winter and 9-22 hrs in summer.
Adults $32, children $28 Tel: 407/351-3600

Universal Studios Florida – Universal Studios Plaza, Orlando
This rival to Disney-MGM Studios Theme Park bills itself as the largest working motion picture and television studio complex outside Hollywood. A joint venture between MCA and Rank Organisation PLC, Universal opened its 444 acres southwest of Orlando in 1990.

The studio tour features 13 thrill rides and shows based on motion pictures such as "King Kong", "E.T." and "Ghostbusters".

Universal's presentation also includes a walk-through backlot, with set locations ranging from a New England village and a San Francisco street to Hollywood Boulevard and a New York neighbourhood.

More than 40 restaurants and shops include the Studio Stars Restaurant, Schwab's Pharmacy and Mel's Drive-in (from "American Graffiti").

Nickelodeon Studios are producing many of their popular children's television programmes at Universal. Along with production of movies and commercials, the agreement means visitors will always be able to see actual film-making underway.
Open from 9 a.m., and closing hours vary seasonally.
Adults $35, children $27.56. Two-day ticket: Adults $56.18, children $44.52. Tel: 407/363-8200

Water Mania, Kissimmee
Located on US 192 near Walt Disney World, Water Mania has more to offer than just water rides. New is the 8,100 square foot Maze that challenges visitors to find four different flags, then exit with the fastest time. The Big Chipper, an 18-hole miniature golf course, and The Little Chipper, a 12-hole putt-putt course for children, have also been added.

On the "Anaconda" slide, visitors twist and turn 400 feet down a water filled chute. Smaller children can enjoy the "Rain Forest" – a children's section featuring kid-sized slides, fountains, water guns and jungle characters. There are picnic facilities and a white sand beach.
Open March through November 9-17 hrs, extended in June through August until 21 hrs.
Adults $18, children $16. Tel: 396-2626

Wet'n'Wild – 6200 International Drive, Orlando
Offers many ways of getting wet among 25 acres of water slides and rides, some of them pretty wild. Newest is the Black Hole, where riders toboggan headlong down twin tunnels of darkness, taking the plunge singly or in pairs. The Blue Niagara consists of two enclosed looping tubes that descend 57 feet. The Bubble Up is a giant inflated bubble with a 90-feet diameter. On firmer ground is a picnic pavilion, and food and beverage facilities.

Open mid-February through December 10-17 hrs, with extended hours during the summer and holidays.
Adults $20, children $18 Tel: 407/351-1800

Off-trail in the Orlando area

Besides being home to some of the world's most famous attractions, the Orlando region offers an array of cultural activities and special events. Here's a sampling of off-beat sights, experiences and places of special interest.

Audubon House – 1101 Audubon Way, Maitland
The Florida Audubon Society was founded in 1900 and is one of the state's oldest and largest conservation organisations. The Audubon House and Center for Birds of Prey has an art gallery, gift shop and an aviary where the public may view many of Florida's native raptors.
Open Tue-Sat 10-16 hrs. Admission free.
Tel: 407/647-2615

Cornell Fine Arts Museum – at Rollins College, Winter Park
A small museum with Old Master European paintings, and 19th-century American paintings. Also includes prints, modern graphics, and the Smith Watch Key collection of 1,200 watch keys used prior to the invention of stem winding.
Open Tue-Fri 10-17 hrs; Sat-Sun 13-17 hrs. Free.

Elvis Presley Museum – 6544 Carrier Drive, Orlando
For rock 'n' roll fans, a collection of 250 items including Presley's 1977 Mark V Lincoln Continental, his bed, guitars and guns.
Open 10-23 hrs. Adults $4, children $3.
Tel: 407/345-9427

Florida Citrus Tower – U.S. Highway 27, Clermont, about 25 minutes west of Orlando
Located in the main citrus zone of Central Florida, observation decks give you a wide panoramic view over lakes, hills and 17 million citrus trees. Tour the packing plant, and ride through a 10-acre lot planted with different varieties of citrus. Afterwards there's a chance to buy marmalade.
Open 8-18 hrs. Adults $3, children $2, under-10s free.

Florida Silver Springs – 5656 N.E. Silver Springs Blvd., Silver Springs
Located about 70 miles northwest of Orlando, close to Ocala and the Ocala National Forest. A theme park famous for its glass-bottom boat rides and jungle cruise past animals in their natural settings. A Jeep Safari transporting visitors in zebra-striped vehicles through habitats of more than 60 species of animals. Watch for

monkeys, deer, wild turkeys, alligators, wild boar, wallabies and a two-toed sloth. Wild Waters, a family water playground, operates from late March till early September. There's also a Vintage Car display.
Open 9-17 hrs. Adults $21.15, children $16.

Lakeridge Winery & Vineyards – in Clermont 20 miles west of Orlando
Gives daily tours and tastings of its Florida wines based on premium wine grapes. Lakeridge is among citrus growers who have turned to other crops in the wake of three recent freezes. The free tour operates Mon-Sat 10-18 hrs and Sun 12-18 hrs.

Gatorland – 14501 South Orange Blossom Trail, Orlando
Located on US 441 between Orlando and Kissimmee, Gatorland is Florida's largest alligator farm, 35 acres with breeding pens, nurseries and rearing ponds. The resident total is around 5,000 alligators and crocodiles. There are daily Gator shows, and visitors can go walkabout in a cypress swamp. Some of the alligators end up as leather bags.
Open 8-19 hrs during summer and till 18 hrs in winter.
Adults $10.55, children $7.37. Tel: 407/855-5496

Grand Romance – port of Sanford, Monroe Harbor Marina, 20 minutes north of Orlando
This replica of a turn-of-the-century sidewheeler riverboat sails on luncheon and dinner-dance cruises on the St. Johns River. Two and four day cruises with overnight accommodation ashore are also available.
Tel: toll free 800/423-7401

Leu Botanical Gardens – 1730 North Forest Ave, Orlando
Fifty-five acres of magnificent lakeside gardens with a vintage 1910 farmhouse museum that reflects the lifestyle of the affluent farmers who lived here 1910–1930.
Open Tue-Sat 10-16 hrs; Sun-Mon 13-16 hrs.
Adults $3, children $1 Tel: 407/849-2620

Morse Museum of American Art – just off Park Avenue at 133 Welbourne Avenue, Winter Park
This museum contains an impressive collection of Tiffany art nouveau from the estate of Louis Comfort Tiffany. Paintings, stained glass windows, jewellery, lamps and other art objects are on display.

The museum is based on more than 4,000 items, mostly salvaged from the charred ruins of Tiffany's art nouveau mansion on Long Island. Exhibits often include other acclaimed American artists.

Open Tue-Sat 9.30-16.00 hrs; Sun 13-16 hrs.
Adults $2.50, students $1. Tel: 407/644-3686

Polasek Foundation – 633 Osceola Avenue, Winter Park
Sculptor and painter Albin Polasek lived 16 years in Winter Park. His museum-studio home is filled with the artist's most prized works which brought him international acclaim.
Open Oct-June 10-16 hrs Wed-Sat; Sun 13-16 hrs.
Free Tel: 407/647-6294

Railroad Museum – 101 South Boyd Street, Winter Garden
Dating from 1913, this train museum is the former Tavares & Gulf Railroad Depot. It has been restored in exacting detail and visitors are welcome to browse. The museum is open Sundays from 14-17 hrs. Admission is free, but check exact times.
Tel: 407/656-8749 or 904/748-4377

Tupperware Headquarters – on South Orange Blossom Trail, a neighbour to Gatorland on US 441-17-92 between Orlando and Kissimmee
If you missed a Tupperware party through coming to Florida, visit the International HQ for a free tour that includes a display covering 6,000 years of containers, Egyptian times to the present.
Open Mon-Fri 9.15 hrs. Tel: 407/847-3111

Turkey Lake Park – 3401 Hiawassee Road, Orlando
Located in southwest Orlando, this 300-acre park features 125 picnic tables, a 3-mile bicycle trail, numerous hiking trails, two beaches, a swimming pool, a 200-ft wooden pier for fishermen, and canoe rentals.
Open 9.30-19.00 hrs. Entrance $1 for everyone over age 2.

Chapter Six

Food & Nightlife around Orlando

At last count, eating places in Metro Orlando topped 4,500. The figure grows several hundred a year. From fast-food and family-owned eating places, to lavish gourmet restaurants and dinner attractions, there's handy choice for every budget and appetite.

Likewise the area offers bewildering choice of nightlife. Here's a list of some of the better-known attractions which combine eating and/or drinking with entertainment. The shows are all very polished and professional, in best show-biz style.

Church Street Station – 129 W. Church Street, Orlando
Converted from a derelict railway depot, Church Street Station is Orlando's complete entertainment centre in a Gay Nineties setting. Leading the fun is Rosie O'Grady's Good Time Emporium where Dixie bands play, aproned waiters burst into song, and can-can girls dance along the bar counters. Many patrons bring flash to get close-ups of show-girl garters.

In the Cheyenne Saloon & Opera House, the attraction is Country & Western in an oak-plank construction that started life as a mid-West barn. Other parts of the complex include Apple Annie's Courtyard, Lili Marlene's Aviator's Pub which features a touch of French cuisine, and Phineas Phogg's Balloon Works which goes for boogie and burgers.

Entrance to all the entertainment is adults $16, children $10, and pay-as-you-go for drinks and grub. Open till 2 a.m. Church Street Station usually plans theme parties to celebrate local and international events such as Oktoberfest, Halloween and New Year. Tel: 407/422-2434

Hard Rock Cafe Orlando
Opened in 1990 at Universal Studios, Florida. The $5 million cafe resembles an electric guitar surmounted by a classical temple. A promenade occupies the 300-foot neck of the guitar leading to the restaurant, while the restaurant itself covers the body of the guitar.

Hard rock is accessible from inside or outside Universal Studios. American favourites are served in a setting which features both rock 'n' roll and TV/movie memorabilia.

Wolfman Jacks – 5770 U.S. 192, Kissimmee
Rock around the clock from noon till 2 a.m. in a back-to-the-50s setting for entrance price of adults $8.50, seniors and children $6.50. Lunch or dinner is available.
Tel: 407/396-6499

La Nicoise Restaurant – 7600 Dr. Phillips Blvd., Orlando
Famous for fine French cuisine served by roller-skating waiters. Tel: 407/351-0003

Mark II Dinner Theater – 3376 Edgewater Drive, Orlando
Musicals and comedies. Tel: 407/843-6275

Plantation Dinner Theater – Orlando Heritage Inn, 9861 International Drive, Orlando
Offers a dinner show Thursday through Sunday evenings and serves a Sunday brunch buffet.
Tel: (800) 447-1890

Sea World Luau
Features Polynesian Luau dinner and family-style show including the knife dance. Show begins at 6.35 p.m. daily. Tel: 407/351-3600

Walt Disney World Dinner Shows Tel: 824-4321
(See the choice in Chapter 4.)

Dinner & Theme Show

The Orlando area features several not-too-serious themed banquet attractions, mostly costing around the same price for highly professional entertainment with a more-or-less appropriate type of menu, copious drinks included. Try one of them, just for the fun of it.

Arabian Nights – 6225 W. U.S. 192, Kissimmee
Located at Exit 25A of Interstate 4, at junction with US 192.
Eat a 4-course prime rib dinner in a Moroccan palace, accompanied by twenty horse-riding acts including Ben Hur chariot races, beautiful white Lippizaner horses, and Walter Farley's Black Stallion.
Adults $30, kids $18, all drinks included.
Tel: (800) 553-6116

Fort Liberty – U.S. 192, Kissimmee
A traditional western fort, Indian village and trading post, with specialty shops and a Wild West dinner show. Developed by British-owned Mecca Leisure, Fort Liberty has recently undergone a $25 million expansion. The Brave Warrior Wax Museum displays life-like panoramas of the western plains of America. William "Bo" Jim, a full blooded Miccosukee Indian, wrestles wild alligators. The 22-acre Western shopping, dining and entertainment complex is open 10-22 hrs daily.

The dinner-theatre deal costing adults $30, children $20 includes ranch favourites like stew, pork and beans, Southern fried chicken and corn on the cob, with all the beer and wine you want, served by roughneck cavalry soldiers of E troop. There's a Wild West shoot-out, cowboys and Indians, and Miss Kitty's dance hall girls.

Tel: (800) 347-8181

King Henry's Feast – 8984 International Drive, Orlando
Celebrates the Court of King Henry VIII with the choicest of his wives, fighting knights, magicians, sword swallowers, court jesters and other historic verities. Everything is completely authentic, as the moated castle was UK-designed and built with genuine materials from Britain. Serving wenches start you off with mead, putting you into the 16th century for a five-course banquet, eaten with spoon, fingers and dagger. Flagons of beer and wine are included in the cost: adults $30, children $20.

Tel: (800) 347-8181

Mardi Gras – Mercado at 8445 International Drive, Orlando
Another British import, featuring Carnival from around the world – Paris to the Caribbean – in a stage show backed by Dixieland jazz and can-can girls. The meal is straight out of New Orleans, with a mint julep to set you up, and then on to gumbo, blackened chicken, red beans and jambalaya and similar creole-cuisine mysteries. Standard price for the all-in deal – adults $30, children $20.

Tel: (800) 347-8181

Medieval Times – 4510 W. U.S. 192, Kissimmee-St. Cloud
Another totally authentic medieval banquet in an 11th-century castle built several years ago with a banqueting hall lit by floodlights. Amid a fanfare of trumpets, knights gallop out and display superb horsemanship in a programme of jousting and combat. Cheer on your favourite champion for a knight to remember. Cost is around the same price as the competition – adults $28, children $20.

The complex also features a medieval village, with millers, potters and blacksmiths to give demonstrations;

and a medieval jail, dungeons and torture chamber. Admission to the Medieval Life village, without taking the dinner-show, costs adults $6, children $3. Open 13-20 hrs Jan-Aug; 16-20 hrs Sept-Dec. Tel: (800) 327-4024

The theatre and concert scene

Depending on the season, a variety of performances are given by the Shakespeare Festival, Florida Symphony Orchestra, Southern Ballet, and the Orlando Opera Company.

For information on What's On, consult The Orlando Sentinel. The Sentinel's Calendar section, published in Friday editions, lists art shows, plays, performances by visiting artists and other arts and cultural events for the coming week.

Chapter Seven

Daytona Beach and the Space Coast

Only an hour's drive from Orlando, and you can reach Daytona Beach or the Space Coast. That coastal region features the most extreme contrasts. Brevard County, stretching from the Canaveral National Seashore to Sebastian Inlet features 70 miles of superb beaches that offer every watersport known to man. Yet right alongside all the space age high technology of Cape Canaveral are nature reserves that provide sanctuary to some of America's rarest wildlife.

Any point between Daytona Beach and the southern end of the Space Coast is easily reached on a day trip from Orlando. If you're travelling on a self-drive deal without pre-arranged accommodation, it's easy to stay overnight at any of the seaside resorts that take your fancy.

Let's survey the potential, starting with Daytona Beach and working south along highway A1A which closely follows the shoreline.

Daytona Beach

Daytona Beach, located 53 miles from Orlando on the central east coast, combines 23 miles of white-sand beaches with easy access to Florida's big attractions. It's the only resort in Florida which permits driving on the beach. During daytime cars are allowed along an 18-mile stretch of the hard-packed sand for a $3 charge per vehicle, speed limit 10 mph. At low tide the beach is 150 yards wide, leaving plenty of room for sunbathing or picnicking.

So it's easy to choose your spot – from near-total seclusion, to the most lively and crowded areas of beach. Floats, umbrellas, beach cruiser bicycles and motorbikes can easily be rented, and vendors provide everything from hot dogs to beach towels and T-shirts.

Downtown by Main Street, a gondola skyride carries visitors high over the Pier for a bird's-eye view of the Boardwalk amusement park area featuring a Mardi Gras Fun Center – Florida's answer to Coney Island – bandstand, miniature golf, arcades, snack foods and a 176-foot Space Needle. The resort area is a water sports paradise. Sailing, surfing and jet skiing are popular, with championship competitions throughout the year.

Just a short distance back from the ocean, the parallel Halifax River or Intracoastal Waterway also offers numerous waterborne activities. Sailboats, jet skis and sailboards are available by the hour. Power boats can be rented for waterskiing or just cruising the river.

The *Dixie Queen* Riverboat offers relaxing sightseeing, sunset and dinner cruises. Modelled after a turn-of-the-century paddlewheeler, the vessel can accommodate up to 500 people. Schools of dolphins often tag along.

Deep-sea fishing charters depart from several marinas daily. A half-day trip costs from $25 per adult, to include bait and tackle necessary to catch "the big ones". Boat captains take their passengers to favoured fishing spots to catch red snapper, grouper and other native fish.

Birth of speed

Daytona Beach is even more famous for land sports. Early motor car pioneers like Louis Chevrolet and Henry Ford enjoyed their leisure time in the Florida sun. They found that the hard-packed sand, gentle slope and wide expanse of the beach was a perfect proving ground for early auto racing, better for driving than most roads. Ormond Beach, the Resort Area's northernmost community, became known as the "Birthplace of Speed".

When automobiles were first raced here, the speeds were incredible. In 1902 they reached an unprecedented 57 mph. The last land speed record set on the beach was in 1935 when Sir Malcolm Campbell drove his rocket-powered car at 276 mph.

In later years, stock car racers began to compete on an oval track along the beach near Ponce Inlet, and racing fans came from around the world to watch. In 1959, as cars became faster and crowds grew larger, racing moved to the high-banked 2.5-mile oval track known today as the Daytona International Speedway.

One of America's finest racing facilities, the Speedway hosts the world-famous Daytona 500 and the Pepsi 400. More than 350,000 people attend a series of formula and stock car races during "Speed Weeks" each February. That's when it's really tough to find accommodation.

Major motorcycle races are staged in both March and October, while stock car racing returns in July. At slightly slower speeds, but equally exciting, go-carts zoom past grandstand crowds during the week following Christmas each year.

During the rest of the year, automotive research and development takes over. Car manufacturers, tyre companies and racing teams utilise the track between race meetings. The grandstands are often freely opened to the public, and visitors can catch a glimpse of the sport's big names and fastest machines. Tours of the facilities and pit area are offered when the track's not in action, Mon-Fri

9-17 hrs. Adults $2, kids free.

For enthusiasts who want to trace the rich history of auto racing in Daytona Beach, memorabilia can be found at both the **Birthplace of Speed Museum** in Ormond Beach and at the **Halifax Historical Museum** in downtown Daytona Beach.

The area's historic love affair with the automobile is still evident, with staging of antique and classic car shows throughout the year. The Turkey Rod Run, a vintage car event, is held inside the Speedway in November.

Billed as the world's fastest sport, Jai Alai is another spectator activity, found at the fronton close to the Speedway. Try to find some kind person to explain the rules. Betting is permitted – likewise at the Kennel Club in the same area, where they have greyhound racing.

Other cultural activities are also held year-round. Symphony orchestras play regularly, with the London Symphony Orchestra appearing alternate years at the Peabody Auditorium. During summer months, free concerts are given in the Oceanfront Park.

At the **Museum of Arts and Sciences** on Tuscawilla Park Reserve is the world's largest collection of pre-revolutionary Cuban art and sculpture outside of Cuba. Much of the art was brought to Daytona Beach by former Cuban president Batista who maintained a holiday hideaway in the area. A wing of the museum is devoted to "Arts in America 1750–1900", and there's a sculpture garden and nature trails. The skeleton of a Giant Ground Sloth dates from 150,000 years pre-Space Age.
Open Tue-Fri 9-16 hrs; Sat 12-17 hrs. Adults $2, children 50 cents.

Culture vultures can also visit **The Casements** at 25 Riverside Drive in Ormond Beach. This was the winter home of American multi-millionaire John D. Rockefeller during the early part of the century. He built the house mainly through irritation at being presented with a padded bill at the hotel across the street. The house is now owned by the city, using it as a cultural centre for poetry readings, and art shows which change monthly. The adjoining river-front Rockefeller Gardens have also been restored.

For nature lovers there are many parks and wildlife areas in the region. **Tomoka State Park**, north of Ormond Beach, was once home to the Timucua Indians. Today, visitors can walk beneath ancient oaks that shaded the huts of the Indians nearly 400 years ago; or explore the marshes and tidal creeks in canoes. The scenic state park is all set for fishing, hiking and boating. Escorted boat trips along the Tomoka River are also available.

For colourful shopping two open markets are held each weekend. The Farmers Market, held in downtown Daytona Beach on City Island, features fresh produce, citrus and seafood. The Daytona Flea Market is a bargain hunter's dream with everything from food to clothing and antiques.

Serious shoppers should take time to browse the 40 acres of malls and shopping centres located on US 92 at Interstate 95. They feature a complete range of stores, ranging from major department stores to small specialty shops.

Nightlife is not lacking either. Top name entertainers appear regularly at the Ocean Center, while there are also numerous nightclubs along the beach and the mainland. From reggae to disco to jazz, the range of entertainment is endless.

Space Coast

Merritt Island National Wildlife Refuge

Ever since its gradual emergence from the sea, about one million years before Space Age, Merritt Island has remained a unique natural area. For 25 miles, this barrier island protects Florida's east coast from wave and wind. Its climate enables many temperate and subtropical plants to intermingle and provides habitat for a great variety of wildlife.

The 220-square mile Merritt Island National Wildlife Refuge is unsurpassed as a sanctuary for more than 310 species of birds, 25 of mammals, and 65 of amphibians and reptiles.

Its open water is the winter home of 23 varieties of migratory waterfowl and provides year-round living for great blue herons, egrets, woodstorks, cormorants, brown pelicans and others. Patient birdwatchers might see the majestic flight of the US symbol, the American bald eagle.

The buff-coloured beaches backed by sand dunes serve as nesting sites for giant loggerhead and green sea turtles during summer nights. By morning, only a bulldozer-like track remains as silent testimony to their existence. Whales and dolphins are occasionally sighted offshore.

Merritt Island's earliest known human inhabitants were aboriginal Indians. Burial mounds and shell middens remain as evidence of their life-style along the shores of Mosquito Lagoon.

Approximately 2,500 of the refuge's 92,000 acres are managed as citrus groves that form part of the Indian River fruit industry. The Reserve shares a common boundary with NASA's John F. Kennedy Space Center.

Spaceport USA

This must rate as the most popular and exciting day trip out of Orlando, and is probably most visitors' first view of the Florida coastline. Take the Beeline Expressway, US 528, drive across a broad expanse of Indian River by the NASA Causeway, and follow signs to Spaceport. Then you arrive on Merritt Island, where the facilities include a NASA Industrial Area, the Vehicle Assembly Building

(VAB for short) and Spaceport USA. North is the Wildlife Refuge.

Spaceport is marked by a line of rockets, like minarets pointing the way to Heaven, as though America has suddenly been converted to Islam. There's an enormous car park, and another for coaches. Spaceport gets 3 million visitors a year, second only to Mickey Mouse.

Spaceport parking is free, as is admission to all indoor exhibits, including an art gallery, "Satellites and You" (a 55 minute journey through a simulated space station), and a 27-minute movie, "The Boy from Mars". That film is a view of how life might be in mid-21st century. It is screened in the 500-seat Galaxy theatre at 30-minute intervals from 10.50 to 16.20 hrs daily.

Outdoors are the Rocket Garden and a space shuttle replica. An Astronauts Memorial commemorates American spacemen who lost their lives. The 42-foot polished granite monument has a rotating "space mirror" which throws the men's names into the sky so they appear to float among the clouds.

Reckon 2 or 3 hours to work through the Visitor Centre at no charge. The only outgoings are for the IMAX movie and the 2-hour bus tour. So plan most of the day for a complete round-up. You can eat at the Lunch-Pad Restaurant, or the Orbit Cafeteria. For a quick snack, go into Orbit and come back to earth with a hot dog and a doughnut.

Don't miss the IMAX Theater for a 37-minute film called "The Dream is Alive". It's projected onto an enormous curved screen which replicates the astronaut experience from training, through to the awesome power of a launch, and into space for a god-like view of Earth 280 miles up, and thence to a moon landing. The movie ride costs $4, or $2 for children, worth every penny. The photography is stunning. IMAX's newest addition is "The Blue Planet", in which NASA astronauts orbiting the earth aimed their cameras at the environmental impact of pollution.

To visit the launch complex, you can't wander around loose. Instead, queue at the Visitor Centre for well-organised 2-hour double-decker bus tours that cost $7 for adults, and $4 for children. You can choose Red tour or Blue tour, which follow different itineraries. Most visitors prefer to go Red.

Halts are made at the location where moon astronauts were trained, with replicas of their space vehicles and an audio-visual commentary on the project. There are photo-stops for clear but middle-distance views of the massive launch pad installations. You really need a telephoto lens.

Afterwards, close to the Vehicle Assembly Building, you can walk around the Apollo spacecraft exhibit, with a 364-ft Saturn V rocket laid on its side and dissected into its separated modules.

Spaceport is open daily 9-18 hrs except Christmas and on launch days. For general information, call 407/452-2121; or call free on 800/432-2153 for launch schedules.

In neighbouring Titusville on NASA Parkway is the **United States Astronaut Hall of Fame** which showcases America's first astronauts from their early trainee days through their missions on the Mercury programmes. Open 9 a.m.-dusk. Adults $7, children $5.

Indian River Lagoon, the most diverse estuary in the United States, is a delicate mixture of salt and freshwater that extends for 160 miles, along 40 percent of Florida's east coast. Nearly one-half of the lagoon's broad brackish waters, which have an average depth of only three feet, is in Brevard County, separated from the Atlantic by a barrier island system, served by Highway A1A.

The appeal is two-fold. It's a quiet coastline of small resorts, in contrast to the big-time seaside playgrounds further south. Partly because of that quietness, the coastal zone is a nature-lovers' dream, with ample opportunities for bird-watching and seeing rare wildlife close-up.

Along the coast there are 32 parks, 31 marinas, and several piers. All this water means there's every kind of both salt and freshwater fishing imaginable.

You can sail in virtually anything that floats, including dining and dancing aboard charming paddlewheelers, or take a whirligig ride on one of those infamous Florida airboats, guaranteed to scare away every living creature with their appalling noise.

Serious surfers come from afar to test the waters of Sebastian Inlet, which enthusiasts rank as the Surfing Capital of the East Coast. Water skiing and jet skiing are other favourite on-the-water pastimes.

Underwater enthusiasts will find the off-shore waters alive with exotic fish and other sea creatures. Sea fans in exquisite colours, sponges and mammoth brain coral are part of an ever-changing panorama. The best dive spots are found at Sebastian Inlet. Equipment and instructors are available at many dive and ski shops near the beaches.

Some of the marshlands surrounding the Indian River offer a rare opportunity for a close-up of wildlife. Thirty-seven endangered species inhabit the area, including the lovable manatee – a kind of sea cow which dines off seaweed. These gentle grey giants are seen in all Brevard County coastal waters, particularly in summer. From March to October, one-third to one-half of the 1,200 American manatees are found in Indian River Lagoon.

In May, when the sun goes down, visitors can head to the beach for guided turtle walks.

Loggerheads, greens and leatherbacks begin waddling ashore about May 1st. Space Coast beaches are the most popular sea turtle nesting sites on the east coast. During nesting season, hundreds of turtles come ashore nightly to deposit their eggs. Hatchlings make their way to their ocean home until late October.

Evening walks are held at Merritt Island National Wildlife Refuge. Phone 407/861-0667 for reservations, though space is limited for all turtle walk programmes. In fact they say that reservations are needed two weeks' ahead.

Another number worth trying is 407/676-1701 – The Sea Turtle Preservation Society which offers walks from Satellite Beach to Spessard Holland Park. That stretch south to Sebastian Inlet is the largest sea turtle nesting area in America.

Cocoa Beach

Within view of Kennedy Space Center is Cocoa Beach, with an 840-ft ocean pier rated as an historic landmark. Settled in the 1860s and nestled on the banks of the Indian River, the original village has been restored to 19th-century format.

The end result is Olde Cocoa Village, a collection of more than 50 shops and eating-places along oak-shaded brick sidewalks and cobbled streets. The Village Playhouse, originally built as a vaudeville theatre and later used as a cinema, is now used again for live shows. The Porcher House, former home of citrus grove owners, is open for public tours. Brevard Museum offers walking tours of the village. For Cocoa village information, call 407/639-3500.

Cocoa Beach boasts a recent attraction, the 'Little River Queen'. The vessel is a 65-foot paddleboat making two cruises daily on the Banana River, including a dinner and a romantic moonlight excursion. The two-hour afternoon cruise departs from Gatsby's Dockside at 14 hrs; the evening deals start 18.30 or 19.00 hrs.

For those wanting more time on the water, Port Canaveral, east of Merritt Island, is home base for Premier Cruise Lines' 'Majestic', 'Atlantic' and 'Oceanic'. Premier is the official Walt Disney Cruise Line, and several Disney characters accompany each cruise. These cruisers make three- and four-day trips to the Bahamas. Carnival Cruise Lines likewise offers numerous and regular sailings. Port Canaveral is rated as USA's second largest passenger cruise port.

Brevard Museum of History and Natural Science – 2201 Michigan Ave, Cocoa – traces the history (and pre-history) of the area: from the native American Indians to the 15th-century Spaniards and the later pioneers who settled the wilderness. The museum includes a fully equipped country kitchen – the focal point of family life in Florida, way back in the early 1900s. Adjoining the museum are 22 acres of nature trails.

Tel: 407/632-1830.

Melbourne Beach

A few miles further south is Florida's home of surfing – Melbourne Beach. Although the beaches are much narrower than those of Daytona, the waves are much larger. Melbourne Beach attracts "hang-tenners" from everywhere.

However, Melbourne Beach does not have a monopoly on surfing in Florida. All along U.S. Highway A1A surfers "make the scene" north of Melbourne at Cocoa Beach and Satellite Beach, and south of Melbourne at Floridana Beach, Sebastian Inlet, Vero Beach, and farther down the Atlantic coast.

If you don't surf, don't panic. The Space Coast has plenty more waterfront activities to satisfy every whim.

Nestled along the banks of Crane Creek, the historic heart of downtown Melbourne features early 1900's architecture, while trains still chug through town. You can stroll to the harbour to watch the boats come and go. This exercise in nostalgia is home to galleries, restaurants, boutiques, theatres and antique shops. For information, call 407/724-5400.

BACAM – Brevard Art Center & Museum – 1463 North Highland Ave., Melbourne
BACAM features touring art shows from major collections, and rotating shows from the centre's own permanent collection, including experimental art such as holography.
Tel: 407/242-0737.

Space Coast Science Center – just across the street from BACAM, at 1500 Highland Ave., Melbourne
Explore the mysteries of science and technology through hands-on exhibits. Visitors are invited to touch, activate and explore the displays. Shake hands with a snake, test your shark I.Q., shine a laser light, launch the earth into orbit, blend your own salad dressing, blow bubbles, operate computers, find buried treasure, watch your own heart-beat, incubate turtle hatchlings – and more.
Open Tue-Fri 10-16 hrs; Sat 10-16 hrs.
Tel: 407/242-0737.

Sebastian Inlet – (just north of Vero Beach)
From Sebastian Inlet south to Fort Pierce is often described as Florida's Treasure Coast. On July 30, 1715, a Spanish treasure fleet laden with gold, silver and jewels was wrecked offshore by a hurricane while returning to Spain from Mexico and Peru. Eleven ships and 700 lives were lost, while 1,500 men, women and children struggled to safety. The treasures went down with the ships.

At Sebastian Inlet State Recreation Area, the McLarty Visitor Center occupies the site of a Spanish salvage camp set up to retrieve the treasure. A 15-minute video presents the story of the lost treasure fleet, as well as the natural history of Sebastian Inlet. Exhibits interpret the history of the 1715 hurricane and attempts to salvage the treasure. There are numerous displays of recovered artefacts.

Sebastian Inlet State Recreation Area is open 24 hours a day year-round. For information, call 407/984-4852.

Mel Fisher's Treasure Exhibit is now located in Sebastian. Mel Fisher is a highly successful modern-day treasure hunter who operates a similar display of booty at Key West. Open Tue-Sun 10-17 hrs.

Vero Beach

Best known for its role in the citrus industry, Vero Beach is a popular tourist spot. The Driftwood Inn lures sightseers with its rickety construction, unmatched windows, and bits and pieces from sunken Spanish ships. Vero Beach is also the spring training site for the Los Angeles Dodgers, who play exhibition games here at Dodgertown and throughout the state each spring. In nearby Port St. Lucie are the New York Mets.

If you can't follow baseball, how about polo? Prince Charles helped to inaugurate the Windsor Polo Club, located north of Vero Beach. Exhibition matches are open to the public.

Hutchinson Island

On the southern tip of Hutchinson Island, the **Elliott Museum** was constructed in 1961 by the son of American inventor, Sterling Elliott, to commemorate his works. Exhibits include the first addressing machine, a knot-tying machine and the original quadracycle (fore-runner of the motor-car). The museum also features 14 old shops, shell collections, and a rotating contemporary art collection. Tel: 407/225-1961

The Everest of South Florida

Five miles north of Jupiter is the Jonathan Dickinson State Park – 15 square miles of Florida wilderness along the Loxahatchee River and coastal shore. Rolling sand dunes reach heights up to 86 feet at Hobe Mountain, the highest point above sea level in South Florida. Sightseers can go sunset-viewing by scaling the mountain's 22-foot observation deck.

How many miles from Daytona Beach?

Cape Canaveral 65; Clearwater 161; Fort Lauderdale 232; Fort Myers 207; Fort Walton Beach 393; Jacksonville 89; Key West 411; Kissimmee 55; Miami 257; Ocala 76; Orlando 54; Panama City 332; Pensacola 432; Sarasota 186; St. Augustine 33; St. Petersburg 99; Tallahassee 235; Tampa 139; West Palm Beach 189.

Chapter Eight

Miami and the Gold Coast

Here's the favourite holiday area which most Europeans identify as Florida, with Palm Beach, Fort Lauderdale and Miami Beach as the big names.

All these famous beaches are spread along the long, thin barrier islands that fringe the mainland coast, with access across the Intracoastal Waterway by bridge or causeway. The islands of golden-sand beaches are totally dedicated to the suntan trade, initially sparked by the flocks of 'sunbirds' who wintered here in flight from the chilly zones of northern USA.

Today it's a year-round business, though December till Easter still remains as high season. That's followed in scale by the family holiday period when schools are out for the summer.

Wherever you stay along this Gold Coast, there's food and lodging for every income bracket, sport facilities and attractions for every taste. Nightlife can be as peaceful or as vibrant as you wish. If you're a nature lover, you're within a short distance of a primitive Florida which hasn't changed for the past 50,000 years. The choice is yours!

All the beachside areas are linked by Highway A1A which steps along from island to island. The mainland townships are trisected by US Route 1 and Interstate 95. From Orlando to the Gold Coast resorts it's virtually door-to-door by the Florida Turnpike – around 200 easy but boring miles, under 4 hours. If you have time, it's far more interesting to use A1A.

Palm Beach County

Stretching 47 miles along Florida's Gold Coast, Palm Beach County reaches from Jupiter in the north to Boca Raton in the south, with Palm Beach itself as the centre spread.

History began in 1870 when a Spanish ship laden with coconuts sank off-shore of an un-named island. Some local homesteaders planted the coconuts which rapidly yielded a wild growth of palm trees. Hence, some years later, the name Palm Beach was given to the settlement.

The take-off came in the early 1890's, when railwayman

Henry Flagler opened up the area with an extension of his Florida East Coast Railroad, which reached West Palm Beach in 1894. Luxury hotels were built, designed for a very wealthy clientele. Steeped in this tradition, Palm Beach has stayed firmly up-market, with an annual guest-list that reads like an international Who's Who. Even so, other resorts of Palm Beach County as a whole are still an accessible destination for holidaymakers of more modest means. Each resort community has a stretch of public beach with facilities and parking for the day visitor.

Today, Palm Beach County reckons its riches especially in land-based sport facilities. There is big-time golf and tennis (145 golf courses and 1,100 tennis courts), while croquet and polo are also taken very seriously. Major tournaments are held annually in each of these sports.

Off-shore, there's every imaginable facility for water activities. Rented sail-boats, day cruisers and fishing charters set off for a party in the sun, for all-day fishing or an evening of moonlit dining.

Like elsewhere along the coast, scuba diving is ideal for beginner and expert alike. Hard and soft coral formations make a colourful setting for a large variety of marine life. There are good shipwrecks to explore, each attracting large resident schools of marine life.

Several wrecks have been 'created' – obsolete craft, deliberately sunk as part of an Artificial Reef Project. Very soon they convert into varied marine ecosystems, covered in soft corals, with populations of grouper, snapper, spadefish, amberjack and barracuda. A favourite 'wreck' is a 1965 Rolls Royce Silver Shadow sunk 80 feet down in 1985.

Inland, Palm Beach County includes a large part of the Everglades, and reaches to Lake Okeechobee. Worth a special trip is the **Loxahatchee National Wildlife Refuge** (see details next chapter), with the big attraction of alligator viewing and bird-watching.

Greater Fort Lauderdale

The holiday area of Greater Fort Lauderdale includes 23 miles of broad sandy beaches, 288 parks that offer nature trails, horse-riding and fishing: 500 tennis courts and six dozen golf courses within easy reach. The pet name for the area is "The Venice of America". Real estate was created out of the original mangrove swamp by dredging canals and creating island fingers with over 300 miles of navigable waterway. There are no gondolas, but almost every lawn ends in a cabin cruiser.

Like elsewhere in Florida, history is in short supply. A century ago, the only building higher than a wooden hut was a lighthouse warning sailors to keep their distance.

Today the oceanfront playground takes in over a thousand square miles of resort areas. Reading north to south, there's choice of Deerfield Beach, Pompano Beach and Lauderdale-by-the-Sea – quiet and secluded, making a special pitch for the family trade; Fort Lauderdale – more lively; Dania, Hollywood – much favoured by French Canadians – and Hallandale. Another mile or two, and you're into North Miami.

With 30,000 hotel rooms, ranging from budget-priced family-run motels to the most glamorous of five-star properties, there's catering for every income group. The choice of 2,500 restaurants is backed by the usual range of fast-food outlets. Shopping facilities cover the full range from high-fashion designer boutiques to Sawgrass Mills, the world's largest-outlet shopping mall with 225 specialty stores.

If you're looking for cowboys and Indians, they're just down the road in Davie. Only a short distance inland, holiday business tails off into an area of horse farms and cattle ranches, where residents wear cowboy boots and Stetsons. Every Thursday is rodeo night at the 5,000-seat Davie Rodeo Arena, and there's a Seminole Indian Village along Stirling Road, just east of the Turnpike.

Also very close are the Everglades, where you can go totally back to Nature in the "river of grass"; or take the easier packaged way to marine parks, alligator farms or a Butterfly World.

Fort Lauderdale is also one of Florida's major cruise-ship bases, with regular departure from Port Everglades. It's quite easy to pop across to the Bahamas on a one-day return, or to go on a Sampler Cruise to Nowhere on Tuesdays and Saturdays.

Need one add that every imaginable water-sport is on offer? Best of all, silent water-skiing has been introduced at Pompano Beach, using the cable-ski technology developed in Europe. In boatless waterskiing, punters are towed by cable at speeds from 10-42 mph, with instruction if required in slalom, kneeboard, trick ski or barefoot ski.

For a change of scenery, a 30-minute drive north or south opens up the sightseeing potential of Palm Beach or Miami. In fact, all the attractions north, south, east or west underline that Fort Lauderdale is an excellent centre for exploring the southern end of Florida. And always those splendid beaches, awaiting your return!

Greater Miami

Miami Beach and Miami – count them as two quite separate places. They are linked by six causeways across Biscayne Bay, but otherwise are worlds apart. Miami Beach is totally dedicated to the suntan trade, while the rest of Greater Miami on the mainland is a vibrant financial, commercial and industrial centre. Even then, Miami is still at least five cities in one – each with its individual character.

Greater Miami has Florida's second largest population after Jacksonville – close to 1,700,000. It has doubled in 25 years, and the melting-pot hasn't yet had time to mix the ethnic groups. Spanish speakers – mainly Cuban – are dominant at around half a million, followed by about 225,000 mainly elderly Jewish; then black and Haitian. The city's first Cuban-born mayor was elected in 1985, and re-elected two years later. Miss America 1991 was of Haitian descent. The keynote is cultural diversity, with Latin sizzle in the ascendant.

Going way back in history, a tiny settlement dates from 1840, when Biscayne Bay was used as a minor harbour for ships en route to the much more important Key West. Miami was officially founded on its swampland base in 1870. A Cleveland industrialist named Julia Tuttle arrived in 1875. She saw its potential as a full-blown city, rather than just a wooden-hut village of under 1000 population.

The key to development was the railway. Railway tycoon Henry Flagler had brought the line south to Palm Beach, where hotels and up-scale tourism had boomed. But he didn't see the case for Miami, even when Julia Tuttle offered him 300 acres free if he would extend the railhead to Biscayne Bay.

According to legend, the break-through came in 1893, when an unprecedented frost had killed off the citrus in northern Florida. Julia Tuttle sent a bouquet of Miami orange blossom to Flagler, who was wintering in the stricken area.

Flagler got the message: "Come on down, it's warmer in Miami." His railway line arrived in 1895, to jump-start Miami into the fruit and sunshine business. Mangrove swamps were cleared, and the real estate hucksters moved in. Over the years, the development of Miami followed a roller-coaster pattern. Land sales rocketed up-down, up-down in the 1920's, slumped through the 1930's, zoomed again in the 1950's, and since then have never stopped.

The first Cuban influx came in 1959 and 1960 after Fidel Castro took over. Wealthy Cubans bought land, built businesses and prospered. They re-created a US version of Havana, and especially developed trading links with South America, with drugs as the big money-spinner to feed the economy.

In 1980 another 125,000 Cubans arrived, when Castro unlocked the prisons and lifted a ban on emigration. From the late 1970's a Haitian influx gained momentum.

Meanwhile, Miami had matured into a major banking and commercial centre, sometimes described as the financial capital of Latin America. Quite apart from tourism, Miami supports some vigorous manufacturing industries, including the rag trade (America's biggest outside New York), aviation equipment and food processing. Miami is even a culture-vulture place, if you know where to look. It can rate high among the more interesting cities of USA.

For an overall sightseeing view, park your car and take the **Old Town Trolley 'Magic City' Tour** which departs from Bayside Marketplace every 30 minutes. Basically it's a 90-minute narrated tour, but you can get off and on at any of seven stopping-places to visit attractions, go shopping or eat; then re-board any time you like. The route shows you Rickenbacker Causeway to Virginia Key, Villa Vizcaya, Coral Gables, Little Havana etc. The tours operate 10-16 hrs, and all-day tickets cost $14 for adults, $5 per child. A similar tour serves Miami Beach.

For the wide range of Miami attractions, browse through the listings in Chapter 9; for shopping, see Chapter 15. To get your bearings, here's a summary of Miami's main areas of sightseeing interest. Map-reading tip: all streets go east-west, avenues north-south.

Downtown – The best starting point is Bayside Marketplace which curves around Miamarina on the waterfront. Crossing to the Port of Miami is a new bridge 65 feet high and almost a half-mile long with a pedestrian walkway. Miami is the world's largest cruise port (more details in Chapter 10).

Along the Downtown waterfront is Bayfront Park, with *HMS Bounty* moored by the Marketplace. A style of transport worth sampling is the Metromover – a 2-mile elevated system that loops around downtown Miami at 90-second intervals during rush hours, but mostly every 2½ minutes. The fare is 25 cents. The system connects at Government Center with Metrorail which serves west to Hieleah and south to Kendall, for a standard $1 fare.

Moving south and across the Miami River takes one past the Miami Convention Center which is a focal point for Miami's urban renewal. The skyscraper towers of Brickell Avenue dominate the skyline.

Little Havana – Spans 20 blocks along SW 8th Street, home to most of Miami's half-million Cuban community. Walk the streets of Little Havana, and you'll hear far more Spanish than English, the non-stop click of dominoes from sidewalk cafés, and the rhythm of Latin American music played full blast. Eighth Street is much better known as Calle Ocho.

Here you can buy hand-rolled cigars, eat Cuban snacks at casual bars, watch flamenco, or sample restaurants that offer possibly the best dining in Miami. Some stores proclaim 'English spoken'. During March the week-long Carnaval Miami brings a million people onto the streets for the largest Hispanic festival in USA.

Coral Gables – An up-market residential area of great Southern charm, built in Spanish Mediterranean style with plazas, fountains and orange trees. Miles of waterways weave through the district, which also includes the campus of the University of Miami and the Fairchild Tropical Garden. The Venetian Pool is rated as the world's most beautiful swimming lagoon.

Coconut Grove – Stretching along South Bayshore Drive is the somewhat Bohemian retreat of Coconut Grove, known as the Greenwich Village of Florida. Red-brick pavements are lit by Victorian street lamps, to make a colourful setting for trendy shops, cafes and good restaurants. A string of parks hug the shoreline from Villa Vizcaya and past Miami City Hall and a convention centre. Several festivals are held through the year, though a festive lifestyle continues year-round. The Arts Festival every February is Florida's largest.

Little Haiti – Another ethnic enclave, formerly called Lemon City, located in a sector about 3 miles north of Downtown, bounded by Biscayne Boulevard and NE 79 St. A Caribbean Marketplace features the food, refreshments, arts and crafts of Haitian origin. You'll need sunglasses just to absorb the dazzling colours. As a conversation piece, try their Creole-cuisine fried goat, called *tassot*.

Liberty City is not recommended for a romantic evening stroll.

Across Biscayne Bay

Miami Beach

The most famous of Florida's sun-and-sand resorts, Miami Beach owes most of its allure to nature – great weather and tropical beauty. The beaches stretch for miles, and are now 330 feet wider thanks to a massive Army Corps of Engineers 'sand-lift' project. So now there's more elbow-room than ever to relax in the sunshine. To view what makes Miami Beach tick, drive along the 7-mile Collins Avenue, lined with sugar-candy pleasure palaces.

The architectural style of the beachfront skyline has had a snooty press for years. But major efforts are now being made to upgrade the image. Especially that goes for South Beach, where an acclaimed renovation programme has transformed a sleazy run-down area into a stylish sightseeing attraction.

Venerable properties from the 1930s and 40s have been recycled, and are heavily promoted as part of a square mile of Art Deco District, running from 6th to 23rd Streets. Buildings are every shade of ice cream, flavoured by

USA's contemporary mood of nostalgia for anything 'historic'. Flamingo pink and pistachio green are the favourite colours.

This Art Deco area now rates among Greater Miami's hottest locales for dining, nightlife, entertainment and shopping. Along **Lincoln Road** is an open air mall decorated with splashing fountains and colourful flowers. A wide assortment of stores, boutiques and art galleries line this prestigious street, which is partly closed to traffic. Lincoln Road is also home to theatre, ballet and symphony groups.

At the southernmost tip of Miami Beach, 17-acre South Pointe Park offers a grandstand view of passing cruise ships.

North of Miami Beach are a number of smaller Waterside communities, facing in to Biscayne Bay: North Bay Village, Normandy Isle, Normandy Shores, Indian Creek Village, Surfside and Bay Harbor Islands. In their intimate style, with their up-market restaurants, yacht harbours and sport facilities, they seem far removed from Miami Beach. **Bal Harbour** (spelt English style) is particularly lush, with the world of high fashion and designer boutiques at centre stage of the Bal Harbour Shops.

Key Biscayne – A former coconut plantation, the island is devoted entirely to recreation. Linked to the mainland by the Rickenbacker Causeway, the Seaquarium on Virginia Key is a popular attraction en route, while a colourful range of windsurfers sail the waters. The Gardens at Crandon Park feature winding walkways, canoe trails, picnic pavilions and scenic lookout points, with restored cottages dating from the island's days as a coconut plantation. At the southern tip of the island is a State Recreation Area with a secluded beach, and a splendid view from the top of the lighthouse. If you go swimming, watch out for jellyfish.

How many miles from Miami?

Cape Canaveral 186; Clearwater 276; Daytona Beach 257; Fort Lauderdale 25; Fort Myers 145; Fort Walton Beach 620; Jacksonville 345; Key West 155; Kissimmee 216; Ocala 298; Orlando 232; Panama City 560; Pensacola 661; Sarasota 216; St. Augustine 193; St. Petersburg 157; Tallahassee 467; Tampa 249; West Palm Beach 68.

Chapter Nine

What to see on the Gold Coast

Wherever you're staying along the Gold Coast – anywhere between Palm Beach County and Greater Miami – there's enormous choice of things to do, and places to visit. Everything's within easy reach along the highways that run parallel to the coast. North to south, here's a round-up of some of the attractions worth considering.

Palm Beach County

Henry M. Flagler Museum – Cocoanut Row, Palm Beach
A century ago, the biggest name in Florida was Henry M. Flagler, who built a huge fortune as a partner in Standard Oil, with big money ploughed into railway construction. As a hotel and real estate developer, he established Palm Beach as a playground for himself and his wealthy friends.

Palm-lined boulevards lead to Whitehall, the magnificent marble mansion built in 1901 by Henry Flagler as a wedding present for his wife. From 1925 till 1959 the mansion served as a luxury hotel, and was then converted to its present function as a museum.

Period rooms are carefully restored and furnished to reflect the opulence of a bygone era. There are special collections of mainly 19th-century porcelains, paintings, silver, glass, dolls, lace, costumes and other family memorabilia including "The Rambler", an 1886 railway carriage designed as Flagler's personal mobile home.
Open Tue-Sat 10-17 hrs, Sun 12-17 hrs. Adults $5, children $2.

Lion Country Safari – on SR 80 – Southern Blvd West, 15 miles west of West Palm Beach
A 500-acre safari park with over 1300 wild animals mainly from Africa. Drive around yourself, but a narrated boat cruise is also included in the entrance price.
Open daily 9.30-17.30 hrs. Adults $12, children $10.

Loxahatchee National Wildlife Refuge – Lox Road, West Palm Beach – on Highway 98

An Everglades preserve of 226 square miles, with picnic facilities, fishing boats and tackle, and alligators to watch in their natural habitat. Winter migrants include thousands of waterfowl who join year-round residents like the Everglades kite and the Florida sandbill crane.
The area is open daily 6-19.30 hrs.

Morikami Museum & Japanese Gardens – 4000 Morikami Park Rd., Delray Beach
A museum of Japanese culture, with a 5-acre Japanese garden set within a 150-acre park. This haven of tranquillity also includes a Bonsai collection and a selection of nature trails. Entrance free, but $2 donation suggested.

Norton Gallery of Art – 1451 S. Olive Ave., West Palm Beach
Is rated the best small museum south of Washington, D.C., based on its prestigious collection of French Impressionist and post-Impressionist paintings. The gallery is also rich in Chinese jade, oriental sculpture, and American art.
Open Tue-Sat 10-17 hrs; Sun 13-17 hrs. Entrance free.

Greater Fort Lauderdale

Butterfly World – Tradewinds Park, 3600 W. Sample Road, Coconut Creek (Northwest of Fort Lauderdale).
Opened in 1988 as the first of its kind in USA, Butterfly World is affiliated with Britain's Butterfly House which opened seven years earlier. Now claimed as the world's largest butterfly park, the Florida site comprises three giant domed aviaries with 80 exotic species of free-flying butterflies. Visitors wander amid waterfalls and ponds in a setting of tropical gardens.
Open Mon-Sat 9-17 hrs; Sun 13-17 hrs. Adults $8, children $5.

Tel: 305/977-4400

Everglades Holiday Park Airboat Tours – 21940 Griffin Rd., Fort Lauderdale
By noisy airboat, with visit to Indian Village and alligator wrestling. Operates daily 9-17 hrs. Adults $12, children $6.

Tel: 305/434-8111

Flamingo Gardens – 3750 Flamingo Rd., Davie
Native and exotic flora, and a tropical plant house, with a 1½-mile guided 'tram' ride. A visit also includes alligators, the Everglades Museum and a Vintage Car Museum.
Open daily 9-17 hrs. Adults $6, seniors $4, children $2.50.

International Swimming Hall of Fame – 501 Seabreeze Blvd., Fort Lauderdale
Fascinating for all swimming enthusiasts, and admirers of Esther Williams, Johnny "Tarzan" Weismuller and other stars. Medals, trophies and varied trivia are displayed, and movies are shown.
Open Mon-Sat year-round 10-17 hrs; Sundays October-June 11-16 hrs. Adults $3, students and senior citizens $2.

Jungle Queen – Bahia Mar Yachting Centre, 801 Seabreeze Blvd., Fort Lauderdale
Several options available aboard a diesel-powered replica stern-wheeler. A day cruise costs adults $7, children $5 around the canals with a stop at Indian Village; there's a day-trip to Miami, Bayside Marketplace for $13; and a help-yourself dinner cruise costing adults $22.
Tel: 305/462-5596

Museum of Discovery and Science and Blockbuster IMAX Theater 401 SW 2nd St, Fort Lauderdale. Dynamic hands-on exhibits and powerful IMAX Cinema put you in the centre of the action. Mon-Sat 10-5, Sun, 12-5. Adults $6, children/seniors $5. IMAX only: adults $5, children/seniors $4, under 3 free. Combo: adults $8, children/seniors $7. Call for show times.
Tel: 305/462-4115

Ocean World – 1701 S.E. 17th St., Fort Lauderdale
Dolphin and sealion shows. Sharks, sea turtles and exotic birds on display.
Open 10-18 hrs. Adults $11, children $9.

Sawgrass Recreation Park – Highway 27, 2 miles N. of 1-75.
Everglades airboat tours, 18th century Indian Village, live alligator and reptile exhibit, camping, boat rentals, fishing guides, food, beverages. Private tours, groups on request. Tours daily 9-5 pm.
Tel: 389-0202, (800) 457-0788

Swap Shop – 3501 W. Sunrise Blvd, Fort Lauderdale.
80-acre entertainment and shopping complex. Free circus daily. 2nd largest flea market in US, top name concerts. Air-conditioned entertainment and food court area. Open daily. Free admission.
Tel: 791-7827/800-345-7927

Trolley Tours – An all-day boarding pass costs $10 for a guided trolley tour which includes Port Everglades, The Beach, Las Olas Blvd, downtown, and millionaire residential areas. Drop off at selected stops, and reboard an hour later and through the day. Phone 305/768-0700 for the nearest starting-point.

Water Taxi of Fort Lauderdale – See Greater Fort Lauderdale via the waterways. From 17th St. to Commercial Blvd, West on New River, 10am-2am daily. Call for pick up like a shared land taxi. In N. Broward from Atlantic to Hillsboro Blvd 11 am-11 pm daily. One way $5. All day pass $13. Weekly floater pass $40. Charters from $75 per hr.

Tel: 565-5507

Greater Miami

American Police Hall of Fame & Museum – 3801 Biscayne Blvd (north of Downtown)
An Old West "tramp chair" joins an authentic electric chair, gas chamber, jail cells, stocks and pillory as the newest addition to the exhibits at USA's most extensive collection of law enforcement artefacts. More than 10,000 items are housed in the museum, located in the former Miami FBI headquarters building.
Open daily 10-17.30 hrs. Adults $3, children and seniors $1.50, policemen free. Tel: 305/891-1700

Ancient Spanish Monastery – 16711 W. Dixie Highway, North Miami Beach
Billed as the oldest building in USA, the Monastery of St. Bernard de Clairvaux was originally constructed in Segovia, Spain about 1411. In 1929, publisher William Randolph Hearst bought the monastery and shipped it stone-by-stone to USA, intending to re-assemble it in California. Instead the crates remained in storage until 1954, when developers rebuilt the monastery on its current site.
Open Mon-Sat 10-17 hrs; Sun 12-17 hrs. Adults $4, children $1, students $1.50, seniors $2.50.

Bass Museum – 2121 Park Ave. (Art Deco District, Miami Beach)
An art gallery featuring Rubens, and the schools of Rembrandt and El Greco; also a general range from Renaissance to Modern.
Open Tue-Sat 10-17 hrs; Sun 13-17 hrs. Adults $2, children $1.

Biscayne National Park Tour Boats – Canal Drive, east of Homestead, which lies south of Greater Miami
Over 280 square miles are protected as an underwater park with islands and reefs to explore. Visitors can choose from canoe rentals, or scuba and snorkel trips. Tours by glass-bottom boats cruise through mangrove creeks to coral reefs 25 feet high, teeming with marine life.
Phone 305/247-2400 for boat-trip schedules. Sample prices aboard tour boats: Adults $16.50, children $8.50. Snorkelling $24.50. Scuba diving $34.50.

Coral Castle – 28655 S. Dixie Highway (Homestead area)
A very permanent monument to an eccentric Latvian, who laboured single-handed for 20 years to build this castle out of a thousand tons of coral, as a love token for his fiancee. Then she jilted him a few hours before the planned wedding. Among the features are a 9-ton gate that can be swung open by a child, solar-heated bath-tubs, and outdoor coral furniture.
Open daily 9-18 hrs. Adults $7.75, children $4.50.

Cuban Museum of Arts & Culture – 1300 SW 12th Ave. (Little Havana)
Founded in 1976, the Museum is dedicated to the Hispanic traditions of Cuban artists. The collection features 200 paintings and drawings.
Open weekdays 10-17 hrs; Sat-Sun 13-17 hrs. Adults $2, seniors and students $1.

Everglades National Park – see chapter 13.
Easily reached from Fort Lauderdale or Miami, via Turnpike or US 1 to Florida City, and follow the signs.

Fairchild Tropical Garden – 10901 Old Cutler Road. (Coral Gables)
Covering 83 acres, this is USA's largest tropical botanical garden. There's a rain forest, a rare plant house, and 'tram tours' every hour.
Open daily 9.30-16 hrs. Adults $5, children free.

Gold Coast Railroad Museum – 12450 SW 152nd St. (Greater Miami South) Tel: 305/253-0063
Half the history of Florida is wrapped around the building of railway lines. For train buffs, this museum offers a large collection of historical carriages and locomotives. Weekends there's the chance of riding behind steam.
Open Mon-Fri 10-15 hrs; Sat-Sun 10-17 hrs. Adults $3 weekdays, $5 weekends; children $2 weekdays, $3 weekends.

H.M.S. Bounty – Bayside Marketplace, 401 Biscayne Blvd. (Downtown)
Reproduction of a fully-rigged 18th-century merchant ship, manned by sailors in period costume. The vessel starred in 'Mutiny on the Bounty', made by MGM in 1962. Sometimes the ship goes cruising, so check schedules on 404/827-2703.

Lowe Art Museum – on the campus of the University of Miami at 1301 Stanford Drive. (Coral Gables)
Houses a collection of Renaissance and Baroque Art, and the Cintas Foundation Collection of Spanish Masterpieces. Changing exhibits are drawn from other institutions

around the world.
Open Tue-Sat 10-17 hrs; Sun 12-17 hrs. Adults $4, children free.

Metro-Dade Cultural Center – 101 W. Flagler St. (Downtown)
Stroll through this outstanding architectural showpiece. The Mediterranean-style complex includes a library, the Historical Museum of South Florida and Center for the Fine Arts with constantly changing exhibits and a sculpture garden.

The **Historical Museum** focuses on South Florida's past; the **Fine Arts Center** features major exhibits from art collections around the world.
Open – Historical Museum Mon-Sat 10-17 hrs, Thur until 21 hrs; Sun 12-17. Same for the Fine Arts Center except closed Mon. Adults $3, children $2 for each venue.

Miami Metrozoo – 12400 SW 152nd St. (Greater Miami South)
Rated as one of USA's best zoos, 290 acres without cages (it's the visitors who are caged), the Metrozoo also includes a 1½-acre free-flight aviary with 300 exotic birds. There are daily animal shows, and a petting zoo.

Recently unveiled is an Asian River Life exhibit, with manmade jungle mist, distant drumbeats, a jungle-creature soundtrack and luxuriant plantings such as palms, bamboo and birds of paradise. Stars of the exhibit are several Asian small-clawed otters and a 6.5 foot Malayan water monitor, one of the world's largest lizards.
Open daily 9.30-17.30 hrs. Adults $8.25, children $4.25.

Miami Museum of Science and Space Transit Planetarium – 3280 S. Miami Ave. (Coconut Grove)
The Museum of Science displays 150 hands-on exhibits, with live demonstrations of scientific marvels. The Planetarium features laser shows and multi-media astronomy. For Planetarium show times, phone 305/854-2222. Expansion of the planetarium, and more space for new science galleries, are in the pipeline.
Open daily 10-18 hrs. Adults $6 for either the Science Museum or the Planetarium; combined ticket $8.50, children and seniors $5.

Miami Seaquarium – 4400 Rickenbacker Causeway (en route to Key Biscayne)
South Florida's largest marine attraction features dolphins, a 10,000-lb killer whale, sea lions, sharks, turtles, the manatee 'sea-cow', plus a variety of fish and other marine life. The star is TV's Flipper. There are plans for major renovation of the Seaquarium, which first opened in 1955.
Open daily 9.30-18.30 hrs. Adults $17, children $12.

Miami Youth Museum – Bakery Centre, 5701 Sunset Drive (South Miami)
Special for children, with magic and fantasy to create the excitement. The newest interactive exhibit is a child-size mini-neighbourhood called "Kidscape".
Open weekdays 10-17 hrs; Sat-Sun 12-17 hrs. Adults and children $3.

Miccosukee Indian Village and Airboat Tours – 30 miles west of Miami on US Highway 41
Tribal HQ of the Miccosukee Indians on the northern boundary of Everglades National Park. They feature guided tours of their village, with an Indian museum, craft demonstrations and a display of alligator wrestling. There are airboat tours, the noisy 20th-century successor to the silent canoe.
Entrance daily 9-17 hrs, admission adults $5, elders $4, children $4. Airboat ride $7.

Parrot Jungle & Gardens – 11000 SW 57th Ave. (South Miami area)
These lush tropical gardens are home to around 1,100 brightly-coloured exotic birds, all camera-ready including free-flying macaws and flamingoes. A new animal show features typical Miami wildlife – racoons, reptiles, flying squirrels and more – to its line-up of daily performances. 'See Macaws and Cockatoos riding bicycles, roller-skates and scooters'. The park has also added more flowering tropical plants, baby primates and a petting zoo.
Open daily 9.30-18 hrs. Adults $10.50, children $6.

Shark Valley, Everglades National Park – see chapter 13.
A visit could be combined with Miccosukee Indian Village (see above).

Vizcaya Museum and gardens – 3251 S. Miami Ave. (Coconut Grove)
Considered the finest private house ever built in America, the Italian Renaissance-inspired Villa Vizcaya, on Biscayne Bay, houses priceless antiques and a collection of 15th- to early 19th-century European decorative arts. Built by International Harvester tycoon John Deering in 1916, the restored mansion boasts 70 treasure-filled rooms, ten acres of cloistered gardens and numerous grottos, fountains and sculptures.
Open daily 9.30-17.30 hrs. Adults $8, children $4.

Pari-Mutuels

Gambling on the equivalent of Britain's Tote is available at two race courses – Calder and Gulfstream Park – and three Greyhound Tracks: Biscayne, Flagler and Hollywood.

You can likewise gamble at the Miami Jai-Alai, if you can figure what the game's all about. Admission charges are very modest: $1 for Jai-Alai and the dogs, $2 for the horses.

Performing Arts in Greater Miami

Miami is home to over a dozen dance, ballet and opera companies, symphony and chamber orchestras, and theatre groups. Typically the Greater Miami Opera has been established fifty years, and is one of the largest opera companies in USA.

Seasons run mainly October through May. Thanks to Florida's superb climate, outdoor venues are often used, including beaches, parks and even locations such as the Villa Vizcaya. For a touch of elegance, more formal performances are staged at the Gusman Center in Downtown. A weekly publication 'New Times' is freely available at hotels, and gives full details of the local cultural calendar.

Sightseeing cruises

There's wide choice of sightseeing trips by boat, mainly departing from Bayside Marketplace. Biscayne Bay tours feature Millionaire's Row, and good views of cruise ships and the skyline, Vizcaya Museum and gardens, and Miami Seaquarium.

Other variations include lunch, dinner or dancing by moonlight.

Chapter Ten

Springboard to Bahamas and Caribbean

Once you've made the long-haul trans-Atlantic crossing to Orlando, it makes sense to use Florida as a springboard to other exotic destinations which are then so close. There are numerous options, by cruise-ship or air. For instance, one or two weeks in Florida can be combined with a further week by air direct from Orlando to Nassau in the Bahamas or Montego Bay in Jamaica.

As Freeport in the Bahamas is only 65 miles from the Florida coast, several cruise-ships offer one-day trips with a few hours ashore; or it's possible to stop over before returning another day. At more leisurely pace, there's the chance of 4-day or 5-day Bahamas cruises to Nassau and some of the smaller cays.

On a full one-week cruise there's excellent choice of Eastern or Western Caribbean itineraries.

In fact, cruise business is very big from Florida's east coast. The Port of Miami rates as the cruise capital of the world. The port serves over 3 million passengers a year, with ten cruise lines and 21 ships, none of which sail under the US flag.

Running a close second in cruise volume is Fort Lauderdale's Port Everglades, offering a selection of one-day trips to the Bahamas, up to full one-week Caribbean circuits.

The most convenient to Orlando is Port Canaveral, right alongside the Kennedy Space Center. That's the home base of Premier Cruise Lines, the official shipping line of Walt Disney World. What's known as The Big Red Boat sails to the Bahamas on 4- or 5-day cruises with on-board Disney characters to back the ship's entertainment programme.

For those who want to sample cruising for next time, there are brief 'Cruises to Nowhere' from Fort Lauderdale, with dining, dancing and the chance to gamble in the floating casino.

Anyone staying on the Gulf Coast has a choice of Gulf of Mexico cruises that operate out of Tampa Bay.

The Bahamas

The Bahamas comprise about 7000 islands, of which only 22 are permanently inhabited. Of the total quarter-million population, half live around the capital city, Nassau, on the island of New Providence. That's where most of the holiday action is located, with Freeport and Lucaya on Grand Bahama as the main rivals.

Columbus reached the New World in 1492, and some historians reckon his first landfall was in the Bahamas. Later Spanish explorers dismissed the Bahamas as having little commercial value. It was the English, after the defeat of the Spanish Armada, who colonised the islands.

The Bahamas developed slowly. During the centuries between discovery and modern times, the dominant industries have included piracy, wrecking, fishing, sponging – and during Prohibition in the United States – rum running.

Many Bahamians claim descent from early English colonists and loyalists who transplanted themselves from North America during the American Revolution. They brought their slaves, who worked the early plantations. When Britain abolished the slave trade in 1807, many settled in the Bahamas as farmers and seamen.

Today, tourism is the Bahamas' biggest source of revenue. A combination of fabulous coral-island beaches, the superb climate, and sport fishing on the out islands give the Bahamas wide appeal.

In addition to just about every watersport imaginable, tennis, shopping and entertainment complexes, colourful sightseeing, varied dining and virtually non-stop nightlife, three of the most popular attractions are world-class golf, spectacular scuba diving and casino gaming.

For those who want to get away from it all, there are miles of sugar-white beaches, many almost deserted. Just beyond the manicured boulevards and modern hotels of the primary resort areas, visitors can admire quiet gardens and colourful little villages that dot the main islands.

Dining out can range from luxury-gourmet to pub food to genuine native fare. Conch (pronounced "konk") is a shellfish prepared in a variety of ways and usually accompanied by "peas 'n' rice". Seafood, featuring grouper, snapper and other local fish is also a specialty at most restaurants.

There's plenty to do after the sun goes down. Music is everywhere. Choices range from glittering casino cabaret shows to discos and tiny clubs featuring original Bahamian music.

Shopping? Apart from all the usual luxury imported products, straw is the big seller. On display are handwoven straw hats of every shape, size and texture – bags, dolls, toys – and still more hats, plain and brilliantly embellished with colourful designs or flowers.

Native markets also feature wood carvers (who will

create a souvenir for you while you watch), jewellery makers who use local shells, as well as other craft people. Don't hesitate to haggle. That's part of the fun.

On Grand Bahama Island tourism has evolved in two clusters – Freeport and Lucaya. Each area has deluxe hotels, good restaurants, beaches, marketplaces and casino facilities. The downtown commercial area is located in Freeport. Lucaya is located about five miles to the east.

Nassau, on the north coast of New Providence, likewise has two casinos, a large harbour and two 18th-century forts which were built in the 18th century to deter attacks by pirates and the Spanish. Paradise Island, facing Nassau, is reached by bridge across Potter's Cay. There are superb coral reef formations to view by snorkel or glass-bottomed boat.

Nassau's main thoroughfare is Bay Street, running parallel to the waterfront. It's lined with stores selling liquor and duty-free imports, handy for people who arrive for the day on a cruise-ship.

Very friendly tax laws have encouraged expatriates to settle from countries such as USA, Canada and Britain. The tax haven policy has also attracted many international banks, which have established major branches or even head offices on New Providence.

For brochures and information, contact: Bahamas Tourist Office, 10 Chesterfield Street, London, W1X 8AH. Tel: 071-629 5238.

Jamaica

Jamaica is the 150-mile backbone, 50 miles wide, of a submarine mountain chain reaching to the 7,400-ft peak of the Blue Mountain. With over 400 miles of palm-fringed coastline, and a year-round temperature of 80° to 90°F, the island's economic life has developed in three main waves.

First was the slave-owning heyday of the 18th century, when planters grew enormously rich off sugar, cocoa, tobacco and cotton. Then, around the turn of the century, bananas brought prosperity which later faded under competition from the banana republics of central America; and which slipped still further after Hurricane Gilbert in 1988. Today the sunshine industry is tourism.

The holiday resorts of Jamaica are spread along the beautiful northern coastline, only 90 miles across the water from Cuba. (Don't bother about the south, which is flatter, mainly sugar-cane territory.) The island is divided into three counties. West to east, they are Cornwall, Middlesex and Sussex.

Here you can live out a millionaire beachcomber fantasy, enjoying soft golden sand on a palm-fringed beach, with bananas ripening just outside your veranda.

Serenity is the keynote, with nothing but the rustle of

the waves and the palm-trees, the occasional thud of a falling coconut, and the mocking cry of a mynah bird.

Super-lounging deck chairs are scattered around the beach. Light sailing-boats are drawn up on the sand, awaiting your pleasure. There's a glass-bottomed launch for a cruise around the bay, or a more powerful twin-diesel boat for deep-sea sport fishing. Smartly jacketed waiters serve ice-cold rum bamboozles or Red Stripe beer at the twitch of a finger.

What else besides planters' punch, beaches, palm-trees and luxury living in a land where rum costs £3 a bottle?

There are excellent golf courses outside Montego Bay and inland from Ocho Rios. The energetic can go horseback riding along mountain trails. There is good sightseeing. To cool off near Ocho Rios, there's the challenge of climbing 600 feet up wedding-cake tiers of rock through the cascading waters of Dunns River Falls.

Also near Ocho Rios is the Brimmer Hall plantation tour, where you ride on tractor-drawn trolleys, through working plantations of bananas, coconuts, pineapples and cocoa-beans. Try the fresh milk of a coconut, laced with a noggin of rum!

On a literary note, Noel Coward and Ian Fleming owned vacation homes in the area near Oracabessa. Noel Coward's house is owned by National Trust of Jamaica, open to the public. Furniture includes a couple of his pianos and a spacious mahogany bed. The view from the porch is superb.

Ian Fleming's house, called Golden Eye, was later owned by Bob Marley, the superstar of reggae.

Further east, nearer to the banana-boat harbour of Port Antonio, is one of the great scenic highlights – to go rafting down eight miles of the Rio Grande, through limestone gorges hung with a lush tangle of undergrowth, giant ferns, creepers and bamboo. Each two-seater raft is made from 30-ft bamboos lashed together. In flatter riverbank areas, local smallholders plant yams and bananas, peas and other vegetables, while women and children scour the shallows for shrimps.

Near Falmouth (in Cornwall, of course) is a similar rafting expedition on the Martha Brae, with steel band accompaniment. Take swimsuit for an occasional dip.

For UK visitors there is bewildering variety of tropical plants, shrubs, trees and birds. Jamaica can claim 500 species of fern alone. Let's just mention a few of the fruit-trees and shrubs: hibiscus, vanilla, banana, breadfruit, guava, cocoa, pineapple. The list could continue for several pages. You can see the range first-hand at several botanical gardens, including Shaw Park, the Enchanted Gardens and the Upton Country Club in the Ocho Rios area. Near Montego Bay – Mo' Bay for short – is Tropic Gardens.

Sampling the local fruits is part of the Jamaican

experience. At a beachside snack bar, what could be a more refreshing lunch than a fresh tropical fruit plate – slices of pineapple, paw-paw, orange, banana, mango and melon, topped with cottage cheese?

Often there are evening folklore shows with Jamaican song and dance and a barbecue feast of roast suckling-pig, rice and peas, yam, plantain and breadfruit. Afterwards, try a Tia Maria or a Blue Mountain coffee.

Also worth trying is pumpkin soup; and ackee and saltfish. Jerk pork, goat-belly soup and curried goat are more of an acquired taste, and are unlikely to figure on the menu of gourmet restaurants.

For brochures and information, contact: Jamaica Tourist Board, 1-2 Prince Consort Road, South Kensington, London SW7 2BZ.
Tel: 071-224 0505 Fax: 071-224 0551

Chapter Eleven

The Florida Keys

Here is America, Caribbean flavour. The Florida Keys stretch 120 miles south of the mainland, but are only 90 miles from Cuba. Even though southernmost Key West is less than a day's sail from Miami or Tampa, it's a popular port-of-call on Caribbean cruises, giving passengers their first taste of a tropical coral-island destination.

For anyone based at a Gold Coast resort, and just wanting a day-trip sampling, then head for Key Largo, 55 miles south of Miami. End of the road, Key West is 100 miles further along. Going the whole distance, the necklace of islands is strung together by 43 bridges along the Overseas Highway – U.S. 1, built on the roadbed of Flagler's Overseas Railroad which was blown away by a hurricane in 1935. One of the bridges is 7 miles long, and midway you cannot see land.

The bridges mark the divide between the Gulf of Mexico and the Atlantic, with the Gulf Stream moving along at 4 knots on its long journey to warm the coasts of Britain. At that point, the Gulf Stream's temperature is in the 80's.

With only one main highway to navigate, it's hard to get lost. All the way from Florida City are roadside Mile Markers that count down from Florida City at MM 126 to Key West at MM zero. Key Largo is located at MM100.

Coral Viewing

The top attraction along the Keys is below sea level: the dazzling underwater beauty of the offshore coral reefs and their abundant marine life.

Today, preservation of the living coral reef is in good hands, after heedless decades when pickaxes and dynamite helped stock the souvenir shops. In sanctuary areas, regulations forbid taking coral or shells, or doing anything to damage the reef. Mooring buoys are installed to allow boats to tie up rather than drop anchor on the fragile coral. 'Look but don't touch' is the basic rule for snorkellers and scuba divers. Visitors who prefer to stay dry can still enjoy a breathtaking view by cruising aboard glass-bottomed boats.

Key Largo

For the best possible coral viewing, make time for Key Largo, where the John Pennekamp Coral Reef State Park and the associated National Marine Sanctuary reach 8.5 nautical miles into the Atlantic and extend 21 nautical miles in length. The reserves cover about 120 square miles of reefs, seagrass beds and mangrove swamps.

The well-organised Visitor Center includes the Aquarium Presentation, which helps explain the coral and its natural history. Park Rangers give scuba divers and snorkellers advice on the best ways of observing the living coral, exotic fish, and other marine life. Even aboard a glass-bottomed boat, it's a great way of getting first-hand experience of a living TV underwater nature film.

The name Key Largo is derived from the original Spanish *Cayo Largo*, meaning Long Island. For movie buffs, Key Largo means the 1948 film of that name which starred Humphrey Bogart and his wife Lauren Bacall. For sub-aqua devotees it means a diver's paradise with protected coral reefs, brilliant clarity of waters constantly swept by the Gulf Stream, shoals of fish to goggle at, and even shipwrecks to explore.

Because there weren't enough wrecks to go around, a couple of Coast Guard cutters with distinguished World War II service records – the *Bibb* and *Duane* – have been sunk 7 miles off Key Largo, where they are already a flourishing home to pilchards, grouper and barracuda.

Also showing in Key Largo is the *African Queen* which starred in the film named after her, along with Humphrey Bogart and Katharine Hepburn. You'll find the steam launch tied up at the Key Largo Holiday Inn, at Mile Marker 100.

En route to Key West

Theater of the Sea at Mile Marker 84 on Islamorada provides a maritime entertainment with dolphins, sharks and sea-lions. The dolphins seem to enjoy contact with humans in swim-along shows.

Islamorada is a series of keys stretching 16 miles. Some consider this the sportfishing capital of the world. The waters are an angler's dream with a bountiful supply of blackfin tuna, blue marlin, bonefish cobia, sailfish, swordfish and tasty grouper.

On the preservation front, several wildlife refuges are well established, and a few endangered species have come bouncing back from the brink. Big Pine Key is reserved for the dwarf 32-inch-tall deer, a distant relative of the Virginia white-tail, weighing in at 50 lbs. Looe Key also opens up a National Marine Sanctuary reef, greatly favoured by scuba divers. On Saddlebunch Keys the principal residents are Great White Herons.

Otherwise the Keys everywhere are well populated with innumerable species of birds, including brown pelicans everywhere, and plenty of cormorants, osprey, turkey vultures, ibis and egrets. At No Name Key, cheeky racoons expect to be fed, especially around supper-time.

A great movie star was Flipper, the dolphin who absorbed the tricks of the trade at what is now the **Dolphin Research Center** at Mile Marker 59 on Grassy Key. The aim is to help the general public understand dolphins better. Well protected by law, Atlantic Bottlenose Dolphins now cruise safely along the Keys. They revel in shallow waters amid the sand and seagrass flats between the reefs.

Tours of the non-profit Research Center are Wed-Sun at 10.00, 12.30, 14.00 or 15.30 hrs by advance reservation only. Tel: 305/289-1121 or 289-0002.

Key West

The road may be ending but the fun is just beginning at sundown in Key West. Every evening at Mallory Pier, a cast of regulars perform music, dances and juggling acts in honour of the sunset. These are not professional performers. They are just island residents (and a few uninhibited visitors) who know how to experience what they regard as the world's best sunset. Extra good sunsets get a round of applause.

You'll gather that there's just a touch of eccentricity about many of the local inhabitants of America's Last Resort. Dress is relaxed, like shorts, cotton singlet and a deep suntan. Dress 'formal' means you also wear shoes. Life can be gay, nudist, 1960s-hippy or way-out any direction, and nobody raises an eyebrow. Residents born in Key West call themselves 'Conchs', pronounced 'Conks'. After seven years' residence, newcomers become 'freshwater Conks'.

Much of the fame and tourist interest of Key West comes from former freshwater Conks, or even those who came for shorter periods and didn't qualify for the honour. Let's drop a few names: Harry S. Truman, Ernest Hemingway, John James Audubon. They each have their own house-museum, well worth a visit. Tennessee Williams lived here for 34 years, but his memorial is outside town at the **Tennessee Williams Fine Arts Center** on Stock Island, where there are regular performances of dance, plays and musicals.

For an overall view of Key West and its history, take in the **Key West Picture Show** at the Conch General Store at Mallory Market. This 40-minute film features "a cast of hundreds", as longtime residents relate stories of Key West's easy going, relaxed lifestyle.

To tour the town, rent a bicycle or take the 90-minute trip aboard the Conch Train or the rival Old Town

Trolley. The guided tours cover 18 miles and 125 points of interest in a 90-minute circuit. Figure $10 for the trip, kids $4.

How about a drink with a literary excuse? Then drop by at Sloppy Joe's at 201 Duval Street, or Capt. Tony's Saloon at 428 Greene Street. They both rank as Hemingway's favourite bars.

The Hemingway Home and Museum at 907 Whitehead Street is a Spanish colonial-style house bought by the author for about $6000 and back taxes in 1931. He based himself in Key West for some ten years before moving to Cuba. The house and its furnishings have been kept intact, as if Hemingway were about to return from a fishing trip or from a drinking session and a yarn at Sloppy Joe's. Even a tribe of six-toed cats are still in residence, descended from his original brood.

Visitors can tour the house and hear an informative but light-hearted description of some of the goings-on during Hemingway's residence. In his Pool House study, the novelist wrote 'For Whom the Bell Tolls', 'A Farewell to Arms', and 'The Snows of Kilimanjaro'.

Open 9-17 hrs. Adults $6, children $1.50.

On the same street, number 205 near the Gulf waterfront, stands the **Audubon House & Gardens**, named for the great naturalist who came briefly to Key West in 1832 to sketch the plants and birds of the Florida Keys. The renovated house was originally built in early 19th century by a harbour master and wrecker named Capt. John Geiger. The museum displays period furniture, original Audubon paintings and a complete set of the naturalist's great work, *Birds of America*.

Open 9.30-17 hrs. Adults $5, children $1.

The 'Little White House' set in 2.5 acres on Front Street was the personal retreat of the former US president, Harry S. Truman. It has been faithfully restored to its original condition, and includes his favourite gramophone records and copies of personal correspondence. Truman originally went to Key West in 1946 to recover from illness. He fell in love with the area and returned eleven times during his presidency.

Close by at 322 Duval Street is the **Oldest House in Key West**, also billed as the **Wreckers' Museum**. Dated 1829, it was the home of a sea captain and his nine daughters. To support their life-style, he doubled as a 'wrecker'. The word has a mixed meaning – someone who salvages wrecked ships or their cargo; or someone who helps shipwrecks happen, for purposes of plunder. Residents of the Florida Keys often came into the second group if their prayers for a good storm were not answered.

Ship models, marine artefacts and antiques are on display.
Open 10-16 hrs. Adults $2, children 50 cents.

For a true-life treasure-hunt story, visit the **Mel Fisher Maritime Heritage Museum** at 200 Greene Street. Mel Fisher is the king of modern-day treasure hunters. His expeditions have yielded millions of dollars in gold, silver and varied artefacts from sunken Spanish galleons. The greatest find was in 1971, when his divers surfaced wth enormous wealth from the *Atocha*, which sank in 1622 about 40 miles offshore. The museum displays some of the loot from the *Atocha* and her sister wreck the *Santa Margarita*.
Open 10-17 hrs. Adults $5, children $1.

Finally, don't miss a trip by glass-bottomed boat to goggle at the coral reefs.

Chapter Twelve

Southwest for nature-lovers

Nature takes the lead role in Southwest Florida, and Mickey Mouse is nowhere. The Everglades offer primitive and uncultivated terrain, still ruled by the wildlife of 50,000 BC. Technically a river – up to 50 miles wide and barely 6 inches deep – the 4,000 square miles of Everglades form the world's largest freshwater swamp, fed by an annual 60" of rainfall.

The grassland northern areas have been extensively drained, and the rich peat soils used for farming – miles of sugar, to feed mills of the US Sugar Corporation. If not sugar, farmers grow winter vegetables such as tomatoes and yellow squash for shipment to the chilly north of USA.

Since 1947 the southwestern region of 2,200 square miles has been protected as the Everglades National Park, with tourist access limited to a couple of roads and some designated canoe trails.

Along the coastal fringes of brackish water, where fresh and seawater mingle, islands are formed by mangrove trees which grow up to 70 feet high. Off-shore are Ten Thousand Islands which can be toured by boat from Everglades City.

Adjoining the Everglades National Park is the Big Cypress National Preserve of about 900 square miles, representing 40 per cent of the Big Cypress Swamp. Many birdlovers flock to the Corkscrew Swamp Sanctuary, 16 miles southeast of Fort Myers. Maintained by the National Audubon Society, raised boardwalks make excellent viewing platforms from which to observe protected birds, reptiles and rare plant life, such as wild orchids and 700-year-old bald cypress trees.

The Everglades are best seen in the more temperate months of October through April, during the winter and spring dry season. Insects are then less bothersome, and Osprey, Great White Herons, Brown Pelicans, Green Sea Turtles, Florida Panthers, Wood Storks, Manatees and other diverse wildlife congregate around waterholes.

A northern gateway into the area is Fort Myers – 153 miles from Orlando, or 124 miles from Tampa. Fort

Myers also gives access to the twin islands of Sanibel and Captiva, with gorgeous beaches that are paradise for shell collectors. There, too, is the 'Ding' Darling National Wildlife Refuge, with fabulous bird-watching, and alligators easy to spot.

Everglades National Park

There's only one highway into the southern end of the Park – via US 1 south past Miami, and take the SR-9336 turnoff past fields of tomatoes, strawberries, limes and avocados to the park entrance. At the Visitor Centre you stop for information material, books and a free map. Admission to the Park costs $5 per car, and is valid for a week, including entrance to Shark Valley (see below). Don't forget to buy bug repellent, especially during summer.

The single road slices through the Everglades and deadends at Flamingo, an old fishing town 38 miles later. En route are a half-dozen trails where you can explore diverse styles of vegetation which each supports a different mix of wildlife. On a short day excursion from the Gold Coast resorts, turn left to the **Royal Park Visitor Center**, where there's choice of the Anhinga Trail and the Gumbo Limbo Trail, along tarmac paths.

Anhinga Trail – named after the comic-looking snake bird which spends hours with its wings hung out to dry – is the most popular, and it's best to get there early. Not that the resident wildlife bothers about crowds!

Another visitor centre welcomes you at Flamingo on the most southerly tip of mainland Florida. There you can choose from 12 walking and biking trails or seven main canoeing routes. The terra firma trails range from a quarter-mile loop around a pond, to the longest circuit of 7.5 miles through buttonwood forest and coastal prairie.

Most of the canoeing routes leading from Flamingo take three to six hours to complete. With practical names like "Nine Mile Pond" and "West Lake Trail to Cape Sable", and descriptive names like "Noble Hammock", "Hells Bay" and "Mid Lake", each trail has something different to offer. "Noble Hammock", for instance, was originally used for bootlegging operations, and old cuttings that marked the trail can still be seen today. "Hells Bay" leads through tangled passageways of red mangrove.

Flamingo features a campsite, a motel, canoe rental and local sightseeing boats. The grocery store also sells bug repellent.

Shark Valley

The only other wheeled access into the Everglades National Park is along Shark Valley, which turns off US 41 – the Tamiami Trail between Miami and Naples – running beside part of the Park's northern boundary.

Friendly guides at the Welcome Station help chart your safari, with brochures to aid wildlife identification. There are regular 15-mile rubber-tyred 'tram' tours to the Shark River Observation Tower. That 2-hour round trip with guide costs $6. Or you can walk or rent a bike.

Almost half the Everglades are still outside the National Park area. A number of tour companies offer 'Swamp Buggy' rides aboard fat-wheeled tractors with a raised observation platform. They also operate hideously noisy air-boats, which are banned within the National Park itself. Alligator farms are another branch of tourism, but it's much more exciting to see them in their self-chosen habitat.

Naples

This very up-market resort has nil resemblance to its Italian namesake. It's quiet and elegant and purpose-built (through zoning laws) for the dollar-millionaire bracket – a potential Gulf Coast rival of Palm Beach.

If you're passing through, Dolly the Red Trolley offers a two-hour, 25-mile circuit for $2, with 28 stops at major hotels, shopping centres and tourist attractions. Check out the Naples Depot, now featuring restored boxcars and old storerooms which have been turned into shops. Between Naples Pier and City Docks is named as Historic Olde Naples, dating way back to around 1885.

Naples is gateway to an area of great coastal beauty, and also to varied sightseeing possibilities in the Everglades, including Seminole Indian villages. South of Naples is Marco Island with three miles of white-sand beaches, and a bigger population of boats than cars.

Fort Myers

On the banks of the Caloosahatchee River, Fort Myers is best known as the winter home of Thomas Edison, who came to polish up his inventions over a 47-year period. Historically, the southernmost land battle of the American Civil War was fought here on February 20, 1865, with both sides claiming victory.

Strategically, Fort Myers today commands Interstate 75 north-south – the highway which links Tampa and via Alligator Alley to Fort Lauderdale and Miami on the Atlantic Gold Coast. The wide river leads to Lake Okeechobee which covers 750 square miles of central Florida and offers a canalized through route to the Atlantic. Jungle Cruises depart from Fort Myers Yacht Basin, with a variety of scenic options, including one- and two-day trips to Lake Okeechobee.

Edison's House

Seminole Lodge on McGregor Boulevard was the winter home and laboratory of Thomas Edison (1847-1931). He came to Fort Myers in 1884 for the first of a long series of working vacations, after doctors warned him of failing health.

Here, during the next 47 years he perfected earlier inventions such as the light bulb, gramophone, movie camera and storage battery, and explored new ideas. Credited with 1097 US patents, he also developed one of USA's most extensive tropical botanical gardens. On a miniature rubber plantation, he found that Florida Goldenrod was the most promising native plant to produce natural rubber.

The 14 acres of botanical gardens include native Florida palms and satin leaf figs, calabash trees from South America, and cinnamon trees from Malaysia. Among the useful plants are coffee, tea, vanilla orchid, camphor, oil palm, and bamboo.

Altogether, Edison collected some 6000 species of tropical plants. Friends around the world knew Edison's intense interest in horticulture and sent him seedlings and plants. The banyan tree – a gift from industrialist Harvey Firestone – is now the largest in USA, with aerial roots 390 feet in circumference.

Edison's laboratory is kept in its original condition, set up for the synthetic rubber research that occupied him between 1925 and 1931. An adjoining museum houses Edison's collection of vintage cars and around 200 phonographs with historic recordings. The inventor's home and guest house were built in Maine and shipped to Fort Myers – possibly USA's first pre-fabricated housing.

Florida's first modern swimming pool was built here – for the use of Edison's guests, as he did not believe in exercise. Reinforced with bamboo instead of steel, the cement pool has never cracked or leaked since construction in 1900. Edison's neighbours, Henry Ford and Harvey Firestone, frequently came for a dip.

Open daily at 2350 McGregor Blvd., Mon-Sat 9-16 hrs; Sun 12.30-16 hrs. Entrance $7; or $3 for children aged 6-12. Tel: 813/334-3614.

Right next door was the winter home of Henry Ford, which is likewise open to the public. It was built without a garage, as Mr. Ford never had a car down here in Florida.

Fort Myers Beach lies 15 miles south, via McGregor Boulevard, which is lined majestically with Royal Palm trees that were introduced by Edison from Cuba. Locals claim the beach is the "world's safest", because of the gently sloping shoreline which makes it very difficult to drown. The soft white sand is like powdered sugar. During the winter, the Estero River is home to an extensive shrimp and fishing fleet.

From Fort Myers the top recommendation must be to cross the toll causeway to the Siamese-twin barrier islands of **Sanibel** and **Captiva**, where the two big attractions are bird-watching and shell-hunting.

The beaches with their bounty of multicoloured seashells bring thousands of visitors every year. The area is a shelling paradise where it's possible to find 50 to 60 different specimens in a single day. There's no offshore reef to break up the delicate shells. Instead, the Gulf of Mexico is just one flat, shallow trough with lots of warm and sunny weather which encourage the shells to grow. The beaches are rated among the world's best for shelling, with more varieties to be found than anywhere else in North America.

Collectors identify more than 400 species of shells, from the commonplace scallop and clam to the exotic – tulips, olives, fragile paper fig shells and the rarest of them all, the brown-speckled juninia. Some enthusiasts even don miner's hats with lights so they can arise before sunrise and find the best specimens before the competition gets there.

You'd better learn two local words: "shunting" is shell hunting; and there's "Sanibel stoop". This phrase describes shunters who spend so many hours hunched along the beach, examining and sifting through thousands of shells, that they often find it difficult to stand up straight afterwards!

If shunters cannot find the specimen they want, they can always stoop to buying at retail outlets located along Periwinkle Way. Shelling handbooks are available to help in identification.

The "Ding" Darling Refuge, named for 1920s Pulitzer Prize-winning cartoonist and pioneer environmentalist, is a 4,900-acre tract on the north side of Sanibel Island.

The refuge features delightful walkways and a five-mile scenic drive, lush with seagrape, wax and salt myrtles, red mangrove, cabbage palms and other native plant varieties.

Visitors can see an unbelievable amount of birdlife. There are shy white pelicans, roseate spoonbill (often mistaken for flamingos), wood stork, bald eagles, the American peregrine falcon, osprey and herons. Even endangered species seem relatively common. One-third of the world's population of spoonbills resides here, March to October. Manatee, alligators and loggerhead turtles are often sighted. A sign says: "Feeding alligators is prohibited by law."

Wildlife is accustomed to the sight of human beings, who pose no danger. You can quite often get remarkably close before their nerve cracks and they take flight – typically six feet away from a Turkey Vulture eating a newly-caught Horseshoe Crab before he finally flies off. During an early-morning walk, an inquisitive raccoon will actually come closer to out-stare you.

The refuge is open daily except Friday, sunrise to sunset, at a $3 charge for cars, or $1 for bikers or walkers.

Tel: 813/472-1100.

Chapter Thirteen

The Gulf Coast

Top of the pops along Florida's Gulf of Mexico coastline is the central area between Tarpon Springs and Sarasota. The gateway city is Tampa, well sheltered inside the broad waters of Tampa Bay, half enclosed by the beach-holiday peninsula.

The area was explored by three Spanish expeditions led by Ponce de Leon in 1513, Panfilo de Narvaez in 1528 and Hernando de Soto in 1539. The southern tip of the peninsula was described in Spanish as "punta pinal", meaning "point of pines". Hence the name of Pinellas Suncoast, to embrace the eight resort communities spread along 28 miles of white sand beaches.

North to south, the Suncoast includes Tarpon Springs, Dunedin, Clearwater Beach, Indian Rocks Beach, Madeira Beach, Treasure Island, St. Petersburg Beach, and St. Petersburg itself. The semi-tropical setting makes the 265 square mile Pinellas Suncoast a year-round playground for the outdoor life. 'Suncoast' is not publicity hype. The area claims an average 361 days of sunshine each year. Just south across the Bay, via the Sunshine Skyway toll road, is another Gulf Coast resort area of Sarasota County, comprising Bradenton, Sarasota itself and Venice.

There's plenty to keep you going, for any time you can spare from working on your suntan. An average ocean temperature of 75 degrees makes the coast ideal for water sports – swimming, water skiing, boating and fishing. Within a 30-minute drive from any of the Pinellas resorts, there's choice of around forty top-grade attractions, from museums to theme parks, botanical gardens, wildlife reserves, nature trails and historical sites.

Over 1,700 restaurants on the Pinellas Suncoast offer everything from elegant to the most casual, barefoot dining and moonlight dinner cruises. According to a survey, the average cost per meal in simple eating houses is Breakfast – $3; Lunch – $5; Dinner – $9.

The cultural scene

There are 15 community theatres, four professional theatres and eight museums on the Pinellas Suncoast.

Symphony concerts, Broadway shows, rock concerts, ballet and art festivals are presented throughout the year. St. Petersburg's Bayfront Center with 2,300 seat Mahaffey Theatre and an 8,250 seat arena is the setting for many of these activities.

Ruth Eckerd Hall, the new 2,000 seat theatre in Clearwater's Richard Baumgardner Center for the Performing Arts, offers a wide range of cultural action.

County and community parks are regular sites for art shows and open-air concerts like the Clearwater Jazz Holiday in October, acclaimed as one of Florida's premier jazz festivals.

Tampa

The holiday business all started in 1883, when Henry B. Plant brought the railway to Tampa and opened his luxurious Tampa Bay Hotel, now home to the University of Tampa. Unrivalled in its day, the hotel featured European and Oriental antiques, the finest appointments, and the best china and tableware. The Plant Museum now preserves the splendour of the hotel, its era, and Tampa's history.

Located on the banks of the Hillsborough River, the **Tampa Museum** also offers constantly changing art exhibitions. The permanent collection contains contemporary American paintings, prints and photography, and antiquities of Greece, Egypt and Rome. It's open free, Tue-Sat 10-16 hrs.

Much has changed in Tampa over the past hundred years. The city of 300,000 population – third largest in Florida after Jacksonville and Miami – is America's seventh largest port, handling phosphate exports, citrus, cattle and seafood. It's also a major brewing centre, and has become the financial centre of the Gulf coast.

Not to be missed, the Market on Harbour Island is a festive waterfront marketplace with specialty retail shops, restaurants and nightly entertainment.

Top recommendation is to visit the two-square-mile area called Ybor City. Here, in 1886, Vincente Martinez Ybor moved his cigar-rolling factory from Key West. Cubans skilled in the art came to work for him, thus forming the core of Tampa's Hispanic community. In the old V.M. Ybor Cigar Factory, hundreds of workers used to sit at long workbenches, shaping prized cigars while a "reader" sat on a platform and entertained them with stories and readings.

Although automation eventually put the cigar-making factory out of business, the Warehouse Building in Ybor Square still stands, renovated good as ever. The iron grillwork, oak and pine interiors have been restored, the red brick exterior cleaned, and shops and restaurants added. And you can still buy a good cigar, hand-rolled in the area.

One of the successful businesses in this ethnic area of Tampa was the Ferlita Bakery. The building is now the Ybor City State Museum, depicting the history of cigar making and of Ybor City.

Incidentally, the song 'Guantanamera' was composed in Ybor City in 1893 – part of the campaign to gain support for an expedition to free Cuba from Spanish rule.

Museum of Science and Industry – 4801 East Fowler Ave., Tampa
An unusual open-air facility. Highly-interactive exhibits combine education and entertainment to explain the weather, agriculture, the environment, industry and geology.
Open 10-16.30 hrs.

Busch Gardens – Corner of Busch Boulevard and 40th Street, eight miles northeast of downtown Tampa, two miles east of Interstate 275 and two miles west of Interstate 75. Busch Gardens is 81 miles (a 75 minute drive) from Orlando on Interstate 4.

This Zoological Park is the most popular attraction on the Gulf Coast. Catching the turn-of-the-century spirit of "the Dark Continent", it's an African wildlife Theme Park and home to the Anheuser-Busch's Tampa Brewery.

Busch Gardens boasts one of North America's largest collections of African animals in eight themed sections – Morocco, the Serengeti Plain, Tumbuktu, Nairobi, Stanleyville, the Congo, Bird Gardens and Crown Colony. Typically you can cross the Serengeti Plain by air-conditioned monorail. In the Stanleyville section, "Tanganyika Tidal Wave" is a water adventure that ends with a 55-foot plunge into a lake.

The 300-acre family entertainment centre also includes live shows. "Around the World on Ice" features visits to several countries with elaborate costumes and staging.
Open daily from 9.30-18 hrs with extended hours during the summer and holidays. Entrance $29.75; children under 3 free.

Adventure Island – 4545 E. Bougainvillea Ave., Tampa
Located adjacent to Busch Gardens and under the same ownership, Adventure Island is an outdoor water play park. Spread across 19 acres of tropically themed lagoons and white-sand beaches, Adventure Island features body flumes, inner tube slides, a wave pool, diving platforms and a triple tube water slide.
Open late March till mid-September 10-17 hrs; also at weekends till end of October. Admission $18.

Tarpon Springs

Credit John Corcorus for launching the distinctly Greek atmosphere found in Tarpon Springs. After surveying sponge beds in the Gulf of Mexico in the early 1900s, Corcorus summoned family and friends from Greece and made Tarpon Springs "America's sponge capital". Greek sponge fishermen from Key West also moved to the Springs, where conditions were more favourable.

Today's sponge docks provide Greek music, food, entertainment and a variety of natural sponges. Ethnic festivals are held throughout the year. The largest religious festival is Epiphany on January 6, considered one of the largest Greek celebrations held outside Greece.

Spongeorama – 510 Dodecanese Boulevard.
Tel: 813/942-3771
Located on the sponge docks, this exhibit displays the history of the industry and the Greek divers. The museum is free, but a movie costs $1.50.
Open daily 10.17 hrs.

St. Nicholas Greek Orthodox Church – 30 North Pinellas Avenue. Tel: 813/937-3540.
A replica of St. Sophia's in Istanbul, this neo-Byzantine church features Greek marble sculptures, ornate icons and stained glass. The building dates from 1943, replacing a smaller structure built in 1907 by the community's early Greek settlers. Open daily.

Brooker Creek Park has two nature trails and a canoe trail along the shore of Lake Tarpon, amid stands of cypress, gum and expanses of native ferns. The park has won awards for its layout, and preservation of the environment.

Dunedin

The establishment of a post office gave Florida's early communities both pride and identity. Two enterprising Scottish merchants set up a new post office to boost business at their store. They petitioned the government for the post office to be called Dunedin, a Gaelic term meaning "peaceful rest".

The request was approved and the settlement previously known as Jonesboro became Dunedin. Other Scottish settlers followed. Bagpipes skirl on the first Sunday afternoon every month, and there's a Highland Games and Festival every March.

Railroad Historical Museum – 341 Main Street, Dunedin. Tel: 813/733-4151. Originally a railway station for the Orange Belt Railroad system that dates from 1889. Drawings and relics from this Scottish community's past are exhibited. Walking tours of historic areas are available. Open Tues & Sat 10-12; Thu 9.30-11.30 hrs. Closed June 1 to Oct 1. Free.

Facing Dunedin are two island State parks which are havens for wildlife photography, picnics, biking, boating, skin and scuba diving, fishing and swimming. **Honeymoon Island** and **Caladesi Island** cover nearly 1,000 acres that haven't changed much since the 1500s when Spaniards first explored the area. Both these undisturbed barrier islands are open daily from 8 a.m. till sunset.

Honeymoon Island is located across the Dunedin Causeway (Highway 586). Tel: 813/734-4255. A state recreation area suited for swimming, shelling, fishing, picnics and nature study.

Caladesi Island State Park (Tel: 813/443-5903) is accessible only by boat. There's a ferry every hour from Honeymoon Island or from downtown Clearwater. A 60-ft observation tower gives a wide view of the island and surrounding waters. Shell-collector beaches line the Gulf shore, while bay side is a mangrove swamp, sheltering numerous wading and shore birds. A 3-mile nature trail winds through the island's interior, mostly a ridge of virgin pine and oaks. There's a chance to observe and photograph dozens of native plants and animals including brown pelicans, snowy white egrets, armadillos and alligators.

Clearwater

Clearwater and Largo are the towns that serve the beaches of Clearwater, Indian Shores, Redington and Madeira. Clearwater Beach is connected to the city by a palm-lined causeway across the scenic harbour. It offers all the activities and water sports of Florida's larger beaches, but on a smaller scale.

Heritage Park & Museum – 11909-125th Street North, Largo. Tel: 813/462-3474. A collection of restored homes and buildings on 21 wooded acres. The historical museum is the centrepiece, and depicts the county's pioneer lifestyle. Spinning, weaving and other demonstrations are held regularly. Open Tue-Sat 10-16; Sunday 13-16 hrs. Free.

Suncoast Botanical Gardens – 10410-125th Street North, Largo. Tel: 813/595-7218. A 60 acre garden featuring various cacti and other Suncoast flora including some eucalyptus trees which are 85 feet tall, palms, crepe myrtle and other flowering plants. Open daily. Free.

Boatyard Village – 16100 Fairchild Drive, Clearwater. Tel: 813/535-4678. Located adjacent to the St. Petersburg-Clearwater International Airport off Highway 686. Boatyard Village is a recreated 1890s period fishing village nestled in a cove on Tampa Bay. Included are restaurants, boutiques, galleries and a playhouse. Special entertainment and events are regularly held. Open daily 10-19 hrs Mon to Thur and until 21 hrs Fri & Sat. Restaurants and shops close 18 hrs on Sun.

Marine Science Center – 249 Windward Passage, Clearwater. Tel: 813/447-0980. Live and model displays of area marine life are shown at this research facility. Open Mon-Fri 9-17; Sat 9-16; Sun 11-16 hrs.

St. Petersburg

The claim is that the St. Petersburg/Clearwater area enjoys more sunshine than Honolulu. The Guinness Book of World Records credits St. Petersburg with the world's longest run of consecutive sunny days – 768 days from February 9, 1967 to March 19, 1969.

From 1910 onwards, the St. Petersburg Evening Independent was given away free whenever the sun did not shine. The newspaper ceased publication in 1986. In 76 years, the newspaper was given away only 295 times – less than four times per year.

Facing into Tampa Bay, the city offers a full range of attractions for visitors to the Gulf Coast beaches. A major focal point is The Pier – a five-storey, inverted pyramid complex of shops and restaurants extending 2,400 feet into Tampa Bay. Fine dining, a lounge and a food court complement the observation deck, which offers spectacular views. This famous landmark re-opened in 1988 following a $10 million renovation, with an expanded retail area, a farmer's market, boat docks and two catwalks for fishermen.

Bayfront Center – 400 First Street South, St. Petersburg. The site of celebrity entertainment, special exhibits, performances, athletic events and shows. Phone 813-893-7211, for information on events and ticket availability.

Boyd Hill Nature Trail – 1101 Country Club Way South, St. Petersburg. Tel: 813/893-7326. Features 216 acres of natural beauty with six trails that lead you through Florida's various ecosystems. Wildlife abounds, with excellent photo opportunities on every trail. Open 9-17 daily. Adults $1, children 50 cents.

Salvador Dali Museum – 1000 Third Street South, St. Petersburg. Tel: 813/823-3767. Features the world's largest collection of work by the famous Spanish surrealist. Valued at more than $125 million, the collection includes 93 oil paintings, 200 watercolours and drawings and 1,000 graphics, sculptures and objets d'art. Even if surrealist art is not your scene, it's still worth visiting for shock value or a giggle. Open Tue-Sat 10-17, and Sun 12-17 hrs. Adults $5, seniors and students $3.50, children under 9 free.

Haas Museum – 3511 Second Avenue, South, St. Petersburg. Tel: 813/327-1437. Features restored homes and buildings in a nostalgic setting. Included are the Lowe House built in 1850, the Grace Turner House, an old barber shop, blacksmith shop and railroad depot. Both homes have period furniture. Open Thu-Sun 13-17 hrs. Adults $2, seniors and students $1.50, children 50 cents.

Historical Museum – 335 Second Avenue, NE, St. Petersburg. Tel: 813/894-1052. Features thousands of pioneer artefacts and unusual exhibits including a collection of china, glassware, coins, dolls, shells, pictures of early community landmarks and old newspaper clippings. Open Mon-Sat 10-17; Sun 13-17 hrs. Adults $2, seniors and students $1.50, children 50 cents.

Kopsick Palm Arboretum – 901 Shore Drive, St. Petersburg.
A wide variety of native palms grow in this scenic section of Northshore Park on the city's waterfront. Swimming and picnic areas are nearby. Free.

Museum of Fine Arts – 225 Beach Drive, NE, St. Petersburg. Tel: 813/896-2667. Noted for its French impressionist paintings, this museum also has outstanding collections of European, American, pre-Columbian and Far Eastern art. Special exhibits feature art works on loan from other museums. Period rooms feature antiques and historical furnishings. The museum has an important collection of photographs by American master photographers. Open Tue-Sun 10-17 hrs. No admission fee, donations accepted.

Sunken Gardens – 1825 Fourth Street North, St. Petersburg. Tel: 813/896-3186. An exotic collection of more than 50,000 tropical plants and flowers that bloom year-round. A walk-through aviary features tropical birds. Thousands of rare, fragrant orchids thrive in the Orchid Arbor. Open daily 9-17.30 hrs. Adults $6.95, children $4.

Sunshine Skyway Bridge

South of St. Petersburg a 15-mile causeway spans Tampa Bay and connects Pinellas and Manatee Counties, and thence to Sarasota County. Florida's longest suspension bridge – over four miles long – the roadway soars 183 feet above Tampa Bay. The bridge's cables, like an inverted fan, are painted yellow and illuminated at night. Bridge toll $1.

Sarasota County

Centrally situated on the Gulf Coast, south of Tampa Bay, Sarasota County reaches down to Port Charlotte. The mainland is fringed by six barrier islands that help create 150 miles of waterfront and 35 miles of dazzling, sugar-sand beaches.

Surrounded by Sarasota Bay, the Intracoastal Waterway, the Gulf of Mexico and numerous freshwater lakes, Sarasota County is prime territory for water sports, Visitors and locals enjoy superb boating and fishing. More than 1,000 species of fish populate the waters. Fish can be caught in the surf, by boat or off piers. At 750 feet, the Venice fishing pier is one of the longest on the Gulf Coast.

Located on the bay and only minutes from the beaches, the resort of Sarasota has developed into one of Florida's most cosmopolitan cities. Downtown, you can explore the Selby Botanical Gardens or the Ringling Museum of Art, take in a performance at the Van Wezel Performing Arts Hall and visit some of the most elegant shops and restaurants in Florida.

The 16th-century Spanish explorers of the Gulf Coast were lured by dreams of gold. Of these Spaniards, one left his mark on Sarasota history – Hernando de Soto. According to legend, Sarasota was named after de Soto's daughter, Sara. After two years of searching for riches, de Soto died, never knowing that the true treasure was in natural resources.

Much greater impact on Sarasota history was made by a couple of circus tycoons in the 1920's. That period saw a big property boom in Sarasota propelled by the big-top circus magnates John and Charles Ringling.

Extremely wealthy, John and his wife Mabel built a palatial residence called Ca' d'Zan – 'House of John' in Venetian dialect – patterned after the Doge's Palace in Venice. Ringling also built a museum to house his priceless art collection of old masters and truckloads of Italian sculptures.

Ringling bought up real estate on neighbouring barrier islands, today's St. Armand's Key and Longboat Key; and he moved his world-renowned circus to winter head-quarters in Sarasota. There it remained every winter until 1957, when the circus moved 20 miles south to Venice, its winter base until 1992, but now relocated in the Tampa area. When John Ringling died in 1936, he left his entire property, fortune and art collections to the state of Florida.

Today, Sarasota County is not only a sun-drenched holiday destination, but also a cultural Mecca. Known as the "Arts capital of Florida", Sarasota is the home of the Florida West Coast Symphony, the Sarasota Ballet Company of Florida, and the Asolo Performing Arts Theater. The Ringling School of Art & Design helps art students achieve their potential.

The Ringling Museums – on US Highway 41, three miles north of downtown Sarasota.

Tel: 813/355-5101

The Ringling residence, Ca' d'Zan, and the original museum building (the Art Galleries) are showplaces that combine the architectural styles of Venetian Gothic, Florentine and Spanish Renaissance. The reproduction 15th-century Florentine art gallery displays works by Rubens, Cranach, Poussin, Hals, Van Dyck and many other Renaissance and Baroque artists. Also shown are innumerable sculptures, tapestries, drawings and prints.

Also on the 68-acre grounds is a Circus Museum that captures the spirit of the entertainment business that made the Ringling fortune. In total contrast is the exquisite 18th-century Asolo Theater, a Rococo gem brought piece-by-piece from a castle in Italy and reassembled behind the art museum.

The museum complex is open daily from 10-18 hrs, and on Thursdays stays open until 22 hrs. Adults $8.50, children free.

Marie Selby Botanical Gardens – 811 South Palm Avenue, Sarasota, just off US 41.

Tel: 813/366-5730

Features over 20,000 plants, including exotic orchids and rare epiphytes (air plants). After strolling through 14 lush acres, visitors can view paintings, sculpture, floral, photography and conservation exhibits in the Gardens' Museum of Botany and Arts. A major botanical research and conservation centre, the Gardens are open 10-17 hrs daily, except Christmas. Entrance $5.

Bellm's Cars & Music of Yesterday – 5500 N. Tamiami Trail, Sarasota. Tel: 813/355-6228

Three favourite museums in one stop. Bellm features some 200 classic and antique cars, and more than 2,000 different music machines, including a 30-foot Belgian dance organ, Hurdy Gurdies, Calliopes (steam organs) and music boxes. Those who enjoy hands-on attractions can play the 250 antique penny-arcade games on display. Open Mon-Sat 8.30-18; Sun 9.30-18 hrs. Entrance $7.50, kids 6-12 half price.

Venice

Venice, 20 miles south of Sarasota, is surrounded by water, and was named for the obvious reason. Unlike the Italian version, Venice has also achieved some fame as the "Sharks' Teeth Capital of the World". Here you can enjoy the novel experience of gathering prehistoric sharks' teeth, as well as seashells, along the local beaches.

If you're looking for something else to bite into, try Fast Eddie's at neighbouring Nokomis, where his restaurant sign reads: "Warm Beer & Lousy Food – Come on in, we need the money!" But be warned – portions are huge.

During winter months, the Ringling Brothers and Barnum & Bailey Circus companies go into rest and rehearsal mode, with combined dress rehearsals and appearances on a Florida circuit. Within the grounds is the Ringling Clown College, where sixty would-be performers take a nine-week course in basic juggling, unicycling, tumbling and other clown stunts. Around 5,000 apply every year.

How many miles from Tampa?

Cape Canaveral 122; Clearwater 20; Daytona Beach 139; Fort Lauderdale 235; Fort Myers 124; Fort Walton Beach 393; Jacksonville 190; Key West 388; Kissimmee 76; Miami 249; Miami Beach 250; Ocala 96; Orlando 85; Panama City 332; Pensacola 433; Sarasota 54; St. Augustine 112; St. Petersburg 12; Tallahassee 240; West Palm Beach 195.

Chapter Fourteen

North to 'the other Florida'

Most UK visitors to Florida arrive in Orlando, and later continue east, or west, or southeast. Relatively few think of going north for a different Florida experience.

So what's it like in northern Florida, with hardly a Theme Park anywhere?

St. Augustine

An easy 100 miles north of Orlando, the entire city of historic St. Augustine is a living museum. Known as the first permanent settlement and oldest city in the United States, entire streets are restored to reflect the Spanish flavour of the 16th century. Residents in period costume relive the past. Daily, 9-17 hrs, you can visit the Oldest House, the Oldest Store and the Oldest Wooden Schoolhouse.

Brick-paved streets are bordered by centuries'-old buildings which serve as today's curio shops and restaurants – all protected by the Spanish castle walls of the Castillo de San Marcos. The first visitor from England was Sir Francis Drake, who plundered the city in 1586. Believe It or Not, Ripley is there, housed in Castle Warden at 19 San Marco Ave, close to the Information Centre.

Mid-June till late August, nightly performances are given in the St. Augustine Amphitheatre of a drama called "Cross and Sword", portraying the story of the first Spanish settlers.

South of the historical district lies the wide shoreline of St. Augustine Beach. Half an hour north takes you to Jacksonville.

Jacksonville

Get one-up on your friends. Ask them to guess which is America's largest city in land area. The answer is Jacksonville, population 800,000, spanning both sides of the St. Johns River in an 840-square-mile mixture of suburbs, waterways, open land, swamps and beaches.

The river itself is unusual – the only one that flows north in USA. Jacksonville's the point where all the lake and river waters of Central Florida finally reach the sea.

St. Johns River steals the show as Jacksonville's major drawing card. Attracting visitors and local residents alike, the recently opened riverwalk combines with Metropolitan Park to provide green oases in the city centre. Spring and summer concerts, festivals and gala events are sited along the river banks. The Florida National Jazz Festival is held every October at Metropolitan Park, entrance free.

A sparkling recent addition to the riverside scene is Jacksonville Landing – an imaginative shopping, restaurant and entertainment development, similar in style to those at Boston, Miami and elsewhere.

Twelve miles from downtown is Jacksonville Beach where rustic old beach cottages are still sprinkled among the modern hotels. There's all the usual surfing, sunbathing and sailing. Along the hard packed sands, cycling and horseback riding are popular, watched over by pelicans.

The Mayport Ferry is part of the A1A highway system, connecting Mayport with Fort George Island across the river. Mayport itself claims to be one of USA's oldest fishing villages, 300 years old. The speciality is shrimping, with some good seafood restaurants. The Naval Air Station is home base to the *Saratoga* and *Forestal* aircraft carriers.

On Fort George Island is a preserved slave-trader's plantation dating from 1792, complete with slave cabins. Visitors can take guided tours, $1 per head, on Thursdays to Mondays, at 9.30, 11, 13.30 and 15 hrs.

About 30 miles northeast of Jacksonville, just below the Georgia border, is Amelia Island, named after Princess Amelia, daughter of King George II. The island is 14 miles long and two miles at its widest point, with sandy beaches of almost pure quartz – tiny pieces of the Appalachian Mountains which have washed down the coast.

It's a reminder that the northern borders of Florida are geographically part of the 'Deep South' – neighbour to Georgia and Alabama. Fernadina Beach is another shrimping centre with a colourful and well-preserved 300-year history as a former hideout for pirates and smugglers. Centre Street is renovated as a Victorian-style shopping district.

Three miles north at Fort Clinch State Park, a restored fortress is staffed by uniformed Civil War "soldiers" who carry out garrison duties. That includes the escorting of visitors on guided tours – admission one or two dollars per person.

Northwest Florida – the Panhandle

Steeped in southern tradition, the Panhandle of northwest Florida stretches from Pensacola to Cedar Key, near the estuary of "Way down upon the Suwannee River", Florida's official state song. The Gulf waters lap for miles along a shoreline of sugar-white sand dunes, sea oats, small pines, and bonsai-like scrub oaks.

Unknown to most 20th-century European visitors, the area was first explored by the Spanish in 1559, when they tried to establish a colony at Pensacola. The French and the Spanish were rivals in the 1690's, but stayed at peace for two generations. Other urban centres of the northwest are Panama City on the coast, and Tallahassee which is Florida's capital city.

In this northwest corner of Florida, the summer heat is less intense, and the winters cooler than in the central and southern regions. In this "other Florida" the holiday pattern is different, with peak season during the summer months – shortly before Easter till early September. The big crowds gather at Panama City Beach – a Coney Island playground for Deep South families – sometimes called the Redneck Riviera.

The inland area of the Panhandle is typified by rolling green fields and forests, and abundant springs, lakes and rivers. Along the backroads are small towns that feature local festivals and antique shops.

Pensacola

Pensacola in the most northwesterly corner of Florida is the furthest possible distance from Orlando – 435 miles. It's one of the oldest established cities in the United States and the birthplace of American naval aviation. The Museum of Naval Aviation displays over 50 historic aircraft including the NC-4 which was the first to fly the Atlantic. Entrance is free, 9-17 hrs. When it's in port, go aboard the aircraft carrier *U.S.S. Lexington* – visiting time 9-15 hrs.

Three historic areas are carefully preserved. The 37-block Seville Historic District contains a variety of Creole, Victorian and other housing styles from the 1780's and through the 19th century. Another ten museumpiece buildings are open in Historic Pensacola Village.

Pensacola's white beaches are pure quartz crystals, like those of Amelia Island.

Tallahassee

Some 25 miles inland from the Gulf of Mexico, in the foothills of the Appalachian Mountains, Tallahassee has been the state capital of Florida since 1824. In 1539 the explorer Hernando de Soto found an Indian village on the site which later became a Spanish settlement. It offers all the atmosphere of a Deep South city with numerous pre-Civil War plantation houses and town mansions. The regional farming today is based on cattle-rearing, cotton and vegetable growing, with lumber industry. As a market centre with some 150,000 population, the main activities are state and local government, education and banking.

The Old Capitol building, begun in 1826, has been restored several times. In contrast is the new Capitol, offering free access to the 22nd-floor gallery for superb panoramic views. If you want to see state government in action, the legislature meets April through June. Visitors can watch debates from viewing galleries.

Displayed in the Museum of Florida History are artefacts of Florida's various inhabitants across the last 10,000 years – everything from giant mastodon skeletons to Spanish gold and reminders of the plantation era.

If you're touring between January and April 30, include a visit to the Alfred B. Maclay Gardens which feature 28 blooming acres of azaleas and camellias. It's part of a 300-acre garden at 3540 Thomasville Road on U.S. 319.

Among the other points of interest is the San Luis Archaeological Site. Digs take place from February to May at the site of this former mission and Indian village. Guided tours are free, year-round.

A few miles south is Wakulla Springs State Park, one of the world's largest freshwater springs – an incredible 170,000 gallons gushing forth every minute. There are river and glass-bottom boat tours amid this setting for many scenes of the *Tarzan* movies.

Southwest of Tallahassee lies the 870-sq-mile Apalachicola National Forest bordered by the river of the same name. The estuary fishing harbour of Apalachicola is Florida's oyster capital, accounting for 90% of the annual harvest. That is celebrated in a Seafood Festival held the first weekend of November.

Across the Apalachicola Bay at Eastpoint, 2,000-acre **St. George Island** State Park is connected to the mainland by a four-mile bridge and causeway. This long thin barrier island is idyllic for the nature lover, with pine trees and oaks, wildlife, giant sand dunes, and crystal-clear Gulf waters. Fishing is great year-round: for flounder, pompano, trout, whiting, redfish and – delicacy of the Gulf – mullet.

US highway 98 closely hugs the shoreline from Pensacola to south of Tallahassee. It then stays inland with nothing much to see, until you shift across to the university town of Gainesville and thence south via Ocala for a quick return to Orlando.

Chapter Fifteen

Shopping

Shops in downtown areas are usually open Mon-Fri 10-18 hrs, and mostly Saturday as well. Shopping malls – comprising a wide variety of individual shops – are generally open Mon-Sat 10-21 hrs. Many of them also open Sunday noon till around 18 hrs. The large shopping malls, anywhere, will give you a complete overview of the full range of goodies.

Shopping is everywhere! Roadside outlets carry a healthy supply of traditional souvenirs, such as "canned sunshine", seashells and Florida citrus. Every region has its share of indoor malls, discount warehouses, specialty shops, fruit markets, craft stores, flea markets and designer outlets. Catering for 12 million residents and over 40 million visitors, stores are highly competitive at the budget-watching end of the marketplace. At the same time, there's the pleasure of window-shopping at branches of the famous money-no-object luxury stores from New York's Fifth Avenue.

For many mass-produced goods – like textiles, electronic items, garden tools, you-name-it – prices are about the same figure in dollars that we pay pounds in Britain. Quoted prices are increased by Florida's 6.5% sales tax, which still compares favourably with Britain's 17.5% VAT.

Here's a round-up of some shopping areas around Florida that are worth a detour.

Orlando area

Church Street Exchange and **Church Street Market** – two close neighbours downtown: shops in a 'Victorian' setting, and a group of specialty stores.

Belz Factory Outlet Mall and **Quality Outlet Center** – two locations, close to each other in International Drive area, offering 'factory outlet' shopping.

Florida Mall – Over 150 specialty stores and 4 department stores, located on State Road 482, east of International Drive area, due south of Orlando.

Orange Blossom Market – here's where to buy oranges and grapefruit. East of International Drive, on the Orange Blossom Trail.

Flea World – on Highway 17-92, 15 minutes north of Orlando. "America's Largest Flea Market", Flea World attracts more than 1,000 dealers every weekend to haggle their wares – garage sale items, discount merchandise and antiques. Covering 104 acres, Flea World provides free entertainment. Operates Fri-Sun 8-17 hrs.

Tel: 407/646-1792 or 321-1792

Miami

Bayside Marketplace – located downtown at 401 Biscayne Blvd and 4th Street, on the waterfront beside **H.M.S. Bounty**. This attractive 16-acre complex around a marina aims to reflect Miami's ethnic and cultural mix. The design combines elements of South Florida and the Caribbean, with a terra cotta stucco facade and colourful awnings. Bayside Marketplace is a development of the Rouse Company, well-known for their Faneuil Hall Marketplace in Boston, Jacksonville Landing and many more.

Bayside includes 140 shops, restaurants and the Pier 5 Market that's a showcase for craft workers. The open plazas are a setting for street entertainers. Shops keep long hours – mainly 10-22 hrs, or Sunday 12-20 hrs; but eating places stay open later.

If you're interested in designer clothes sold discounted without the labels, try exploring the Miami Fashion District. More than 500 garment factories are located mainly in the neighbourhood of NW Fifth Avenue, between NW 22nd and 30th Streets. It represents America's largest fashion district outside New York, and has flourished for the past 60 years.

For much more exclusive window-shopping, look at the Lincoln Road Mall in Miami Beach; or, most exclusive of all, at Bal Harbour Shops at Collins Avenue and 97th Street.

Palm Beach County

A million dollar mile of temptation along **Worth Avenue** is the heart of Palm Beach, stretching from South Ocean Boulevard to Coconut Row. Sport stars, royalty and social celebrities patronise the spectacular array of more than 200 shops, galleries and fine restaurants. It's a window-shopper's paradise, but don't spoil it by asking the price.

At the other price extreme is the Palm Beach Outlet Center, a factory outlet shopping mall at 5700 Okeechobee Blvd, just east of the Florida Turnpike.

In between on prices are another half-dozen major

shopping malls, plus the usual local shopping centres. Largest of them is the Gardens Mall on PGA Boulevard, east of Interstate 95.

Sarasota

If you're visiting Sarasota on the west coast, go window-shopping at St. Armands Circle – a ring of expensive boutiques, galleries, gourmet shops and restaurants.

Tampa

The city has something for every shopping buff, in settings that range from the historic to the upscale. For the historic, go to **Ybor Square** where three classical brick buildings surround a cobblestone plaza, with shops that sell ethnic clothing and accessories, gourmet grocery foods and inexpensive jewellery. However, the largest number of dealers offer bygones, mostly in open stalls known as the Nostalgia Market.

Old Hyde Park Village, located in one of Tampa's most "aristocratic" neighbourhoods and along Bayshore Boulevard, combines turn-of-the-century charm with urban elegance. It has a specialty department store, and a good selection of yuppie-shops.

Jacksonville

Another Rouse Company waterfront development, the Jacksonville Landing, opened in 1987, and is a festival marketplace featuring 120 shops and eating-places. The two-level U-shaped pavilion fronts the St. Johns River in the heart of downtown Jacksonville.

Chapter Sixteen

Eating and Drinking

When you eat out, there's no need to wonder if your wallet or credit card will stand the strain. There is enormous range of eating places in every price category.

It's service that costs money in America. If a couple of you dine out in restaurants heavy with foreign cuisine "atmosphere", linen table-cloths, bow-tie service and (most expensive of all) candlelight – then be ready to sign away a 100-dollar traveller cheque.

If you want to watch your budget, do as the American holidaymakers do. Eat US-style in coffee-shops, department-store lunch-counters, drug-stores, grills and roadside drive-ins. In tourist restaurants an average set lunch costs $5 to $7.

The main British complaint is that helpings are too enormous. Many restaurants offer self-service buffets, all you can stuff for a set price. Or try eating in a deli – a delicatessen that sells salads and sandwiches which often can be eaten on the spot, in snack-bar style. A typical deli proclaims DELIcious sandwiches.

Moderately priced restaurants include buffet-style cafeterias, steak houses, and southern-style diners. These restaurants usually offer lower-priced children's menus. Watch for billboard specials, often featured even at the more up-scale restaurants. Some eating places offer 'early-bird dinners' or 'early diner specials' at discount prices for those who start an evening meal before 6 p.m. Sometimes the deal is aimed at couples: "Buy one dinner, get the second for $3". All-you-can-eat Sunday brunch is a popular institution, usually offered between 11 a.m. and 3 p.m.

If you're over 60, or even 55, many restaurants feature lower-cost Senior Citizen menus with possibly slightly smaller portions, but usually more than enough for most UK appetites.

If you just want a quick meal, nothing fancy, there are thousands of fast-food franchise restaurants with names that have become totally familiar in Britain.

Here are some typical fast-food prices: coffee 50 cents; French fries 65 cents; Hamburger $1.15; Cheeseburger

$1.30; Kingsize Hotdog $1.40; pie 50 cents; ham and cheese sandwich $1.90.

Typical American fare is burgers, fried chicken, steaks and seafood. They are much better at salad side-dishes than at English-style cooked veg.

There is great accent on folksy food. A typical roadside inn promotes itself: ". . . where things are like they used to be." There are plenty of Mom's Kitchens where they serve bowls of home-made soup, boiled lobster dinners and Key lime pie. Breakfast can feature hand-squeezed orange juice and home-made jam.

Breakfast is rarely included in hotel or motel room rates. You can have it on the premises, but there's no obligation. If you go around the corner for a coffee-shop breakfast, nobody will raise an eyebrow because you're not patronising the hotel dining-room.

A coffee-shop breakfast is part of the American lifestyle. The waitress first pours your iced water and then offers coffee even before you've decided on your main order. Typical price is $4 or $5 for an American cooked breakfast of orange juice, ham and eggs, grits or home fries, toast, jelly and unlimited coffee.

Evening meal prices? Outside the hotels, an average restaurant can do dinners at around $10. In general, you'll pay less in Florida than for an equivalent meal in a British restaurant of similar grade. Helpings will be much bigger, with more meat than most Brits can handle without a doggy-bag.

In a typical steak house, the smallest-size 8-ounce steak is described as "for a young lady of finnicky appetite." A single pizza can measure one foot two inches across. You'll soon get the message, why so many fatties in Florida.

Seafood restaurants serve ultra-fresh catches-of-the-day, chef's specials, shrimp, lobster (crawfish) and squid. A basic fish on most seafood menus is grouper or red snapper. Oysters can cost as little as $4 a dozen during the October through May season. Try conch chowder, the great specialty of the Florida Keys.

In adventurous mood, you can order some of the mysterious dishes which the American genius has devised – like "English muffins" for breakfast, French toast, or hominy grits.

Sometimes menus take a while to digest, written by captive poets who go into raptures about every item. Often the menus sound far more of a gourmet's dream than the end result. National specialities figure on most menus – often in a style quite unknown in the alleged country of origin.

Ice cream parlours are like nothing we know in Britain. A typical counter offers thirty flavours that range from peppermint, vanilla, spumoni, black cherry, super fudge chunks, blueberry cheese cake, chocolate, raspberry to orange. They come in cones, dishes, shakes, splits, sundaes, artic swirls and malts. Don't over-indulge the kids with too much ice cream when the sun is high.

Drinks

Coffee is offered regular or de-caff. With 'cream', usually means milk.

Early evening, many bars proclaim "two drinks for the price of one" during Happy Hour.

Don't take a 'pub' sign too literally. In a "typical" English pub, customers at the bar perch shoulder-to-shoulder drinking martinis. Waitresses in fishnet stockings serve other drinkers at candle-lit tables. Over the sound of background Hawaiian music, the friendly bartender says: "Just like an English pub, isn't it?" He accepts payment for the ice-cold beers with a Credit Card.

Self-catering

Local fish markets and farmers markets provide totally fresh ingredients for preparing in your own apartment, 'efficiency' or cottage. Load up at a supermarket, and you'll find your check-out bill is lower than back home. Corner grocery stores are always close by for the supplies you've forgotten.

Even if you don't have self-catering accommodation, picnics are an easy option, with superb choice of fruit, salad items, cheeses and cooked meats.

Food language

Bagel – Hard roll, glazed and shaped like a doughnut
Biscuits – scones
Broil – grill
Check – bill
Coleslaw – salad of sliced raw cabbage
Cookie – biscuit
Corn – maize
Crawfish – small lobster
Eggplant – aubergine
Eggs, easy – with soft yolks
Eggs sunny side up – fried eggs, yolk uppermost
English muffin – a small cup-sized cake, usually served hot for breakfast
French fries – chips
Goobers – peanuts
Green onions – spring onions
Grits – coarsely ground maize
Ground – minced
Gumbo – Creole stew with okra
Hash browns – diced boiled potatoes, fried in bacon fat until brown
Hominy grits – breakfast dish of grits boiled in milk or water
Hush puppies – fried cornmeal balls

Jello – jelly
Jelly – jam
Mulligan – meat and veg stew
Pan fried – sautéed
Pastrami – highly seasoned smoked or pickled beef
Potato chips – crisps
Preserve – jam
Raw bar – oyster bar
Reuben – Swiss cheese, corned beef and sauerkraut toasted on kosher rye bread
Sherbert – fruit-flavoured water ice
A side of bacon – a normal portion of bacon served on a side dish
Surf 'n' turf – a combination of steak and seafood
Take-out or **carry-out** – take-away
Yellow turnips – swedes

Some US and Florida specialities

Blackened alligator – alligator meat blackened by Cajun spices.
Bollos – a form of savoury hush puppy that uses mashed black-eyed peas instead of ground cornmeal.
Conch – shellfish which can be served in fritters or raw in salads. There are even conch-burgers. A favourite is thick conch chowder.
Dirty rice – black-eyed peas and white rice: a traditional Southern dish.
Key lime pie – a yellow-coloured pie which gets its flavour from the juice and grated rind of Key limes.
Lechon – a style of roast pork flavoured with garlic and oranges.
Shrimp – in Britain we'd call them large prawns.
Stone crabs – steamed giant crab legs. Fresh October-March, otherwise frozen.

Chapter Seventeen

Main dates in Florida history

Prehistory

8,000 BC – Following the last ice age, Florida is settled by Caribbean groups and by Indians from the north. By the 16th century AD, four Indian tribes occupy Florida – Apalachee, Calusa, Tequesta and Timucua. Their numbers total an estimated 25,000.

The Spaniards arrive

1513 AD – Juan Ponce de Leon lands near present-day St. Augustine and claims Florida for Spain.
1521 – Juan Ponce returned to colonize "the island of Florida", but is killed by an Indian arrow.
1528 – Another Spanish explorer, Panfilo de Narvaez, sails into Tampa Bay and ventures inland.
1539 – Hernando de Soto lands near Sarasota (hence that city's name), explores the Tampa Bay area and then marches north.
1559 – A Spanish expedition of 1,600 men and women, led by Tristan de Luna, tries to establish a permanent settlement on Pensacola Bay.
1561 – The Pensacola settlement fails, and is abandoned.
1562 – A French Huguenot settlement is founded on the St. Johns River by Jean Ribaut.
1564 – The French build Fort Caroline, near present-day Jacksonville.
1565 – A Spanish expedition, led by Pedro Menendez de Aviles, is launched to drive out the French. A base is established at St. Augustine, Fort Caroline is captured, and most of the Frenchmen are executed, including Ribaut who loses his head. St. Augustine becomes the first and oldest continuous settlement in North America. For the next two centuries, Florida remains Spanish territory. Jesuit and Franciscan missions and forts are established across northern Florida and on the south-western coast.
1762 – During the Seven Years' War (1756-63) against France and Spain, Britain captures the Spanish colony of Cuba.

1763 – Under the peace treaty, Britain swaps Cuba for Florida, which thus comes under British rule. During the next 20 years, the territory is sliced into two separate colonies, East Florida and West Florida.
1776 – During the American Revolution, East and West Floridians support England. Bur the Spanish invade, recapture Pensacola and resume control of West Florida.
1783 – The Treaty of Paris returns Florida to Spain.
1812 – Britain, now allied to Spain, lands troops to establish Pensacola as a naval base.
1814 – American forces under General Andrew "Old Hickory" Jackson move into Florida and expel the British Redcoats.
1817-18 – In hot pursuit of Indians during the First Seminole War, General Jackson charges back into Florida.

Becomes part of USA

1819 – Spain agrees to sell Florida to US for $5 million.
1821 – US finally takes over, and settlers stream in.
1823 – Tallahassee chosen as Florida's capital. A treaty is signed with Seminole Indians to establish a reserve in west central Florida.
1835-42 – Second Seminole War. The Indians use guerrilla tactics, the settlers build Forts such as Lauderdale, Pierce and Myers. Defeated, the captured Indians are shipped to Oklahoma, while small numbers escape into the Everglades.
1845 – Slave-owning Florida enters the Union as the 27th state.
1861 – Civil War: Florida joins the other slave-owning states of the South. Union soldiers quickly capture most of the coastal towns, but Tallahassee remains under the Confederate flag throughout the war.
1864 – The Battle of Olustee, stopping an advance of Union troops, is one of the last Confederate victories.
1865 – Civil War ends.

Economic expansion

1868 – Florida is readmitted to the Union.
1880 – In 12 years, Florida's population has doubled to 270,000. The economy begins to grow rapidly. Big phosphate deposits are discovered, and citrus groves are planted along Indian River. Hamilton Disston (1844-96) drains swamps for farming and settlement, and makes rivers navigable. Railway tycoons – Henry B. Plant (1819-99) and Henry M. Flagler (1830-1913) – open up lines to Tampa and Palm Beach. Luxury hotels encourage wealthy visitors to escape to Florida's winter climate.
1895 – Flagler extends the railway line to Miami.
1902 – The automobile age takes off, with world speed record of 57 mph established at Daytona Beach.
1912 – Flagler's railway reaches Key West.

Modern Times

1920's – Big land boom, with real estate rocketing.
1926 – Cold winter and hurricane damage to Miami bring land prices back to earth.
1929 – Recovery, but then the Great Depression pricks the balloon.
1935 – Sir Malcolm Campbell hits a land speed record of 276 mph in a rocket-powered car.
1935 – Railway bridge links with Key West destroyed by a hurricane, to be replaced by road bridges.
1940 – Growth slowly returns during the 1930's, then accelerates with development of war industries.
1950's – Tourism, commercial farming, NASA aerospace and retirement industries all grow rapidly. Population zooms from 2,771,000 in 1950 to around 12 million today.
1960's – Influx of refugees from Castro's Cuba, mainly to Miami.
1980 – More Cubans arrive, sparking racial tensions with Miami's black community.

STATE SYMBOLS: Nickname – Sunshine State. Bird – mockingbird. Flower – orange blossom. Tree – sabal palm. Motto – In God We Trust. Song – "Old Folks at Home" (Swanee River). Flag – white with the Seal of the State in the centre, and red bars extending from the Seal to each corner of the flag.

Chapter Eighteen

Learn to speak American

Thanks to TV and the movies, most Brits can already understand basic American, though the range of accents circulating in Florida can still bewilder. In parts of Miami, Spanish is more useful. Meanwhile, learn American in thirty seconds:

Automobile language

AAA or **Triple A** – American Automobile Association
A/C – air conditioned
Dimmed lights – dipped headlights
Divided highway – dual carriageway
Fender – wing, or mudguard
A flat – a puncture
A gallon of **gas** – .83 gallon or 3.8 litres of petrol
Gas station – filling station
Hood – car bonnet
Muffler – silencer
Pavement – road surface
RV or **Recreational Vehicle** – a camper or motor-home
Sidewalk – pavement
Toll plaza – where you pay on a turnpike
Traffic circle – roundabout
Trunk – the car boot
Turnpike – a toll motorway
Yield – give way

Money language

Penny – a one-cent coin
Nickel – 5-cent coin
Dime – 10-cent coin
Quarter – 25-cent coin
Two bits – 25 cents
A grand – $1,000
Billfold – wallet

Around the house or hotel

A.P. – American Plan – room and full board
Bahama beds – twin beds convertible to daytime couches, usually in an 'efficiency' (q.v.)

Condo – short for condominium, a block of apartments (flats), each owned individually by the residents
Drapes – curtains
Duplex apartments – flats on two floors, separate entrances
Duplex house – semidetached
An efficiency – a self-catering bedroom/living room with kitchenette
Family Plan – children stay free when sharing parents' room
Faucet – tap
First floor – ground floor
Hollywood beds – same as Bahama beds (q.v.)
M.A.P. – Modified American Plan – room and half board
Second floor – first floor
Stroller – folding push-chair
Washcloth – face flannel

Other useful words

Boardwalk – a beach promenade or a nature trail path made of wooden planks
Collect call – reverse charge phone call
Comfort station – public lavatory
Comfort stop – a pause to use the comfort station
Diaper – nappy
Drugstore – much more than a chemist, sells all sundry items, newspapers, snacks and light meals
A fifth – one-fifth of US gallon, usually of spirits
Homely – of plain or unattractive appearance
The john – the W.C.
Liquor store – off-licence
Minister – vicar
Pari-mutuel – the Tote at a race meeting
Restroom – the toilet
Sneakers – trainers
Stand in line – queue up
Tubing – (a verb) – floating downstream in the centre of a fat innertube

Time & dates

US-style dates are written month/day/year. So 7/4 is the Fourth of July. America hasn't yet taken to the 24-hour timetable system. Phrases like 'Tuesday through Friday' mean 'Tuesday till Friday inclusive'.

Special Florida words

Conch – pronounced 'konk', an edible mollusc, but also a person born in Key West
Coquina – a cockle shell; but it's also an easily-quarried yellow rock formed by solidified shells and sand
Cracker – a person born in Florida

Florida moss – Spanish moss
Hammock – a wooded area above the level of adjacent marsh
Key – island, or cay, of coral origin
Snowbirds – northerners who winter in Florida

(See food chapter 15 for menu language)

Chapter Nineteen

Travel Tips & Information

The Sunshine State

Florida is happy to boast about its sunshine. But it can cause problems, especially to the fair-skinned. Go carefully with your sunbathing. For the first few days, severely limit your exposure especially between 10-15 hrs. Use a high-factor sunburn lotion. If you burn easily, a Sun Protection Factor of at least 8 is suggested, but one or two points above that is better. The sun's ultra-violet rays can still fry you through cloud. Err on the side of caution. Better white or pink than lobster-red.

Electricity

110/115-volt AC, 60-cycle current using US-style small, flat two-pin plugs. Pack an appropriate transformer and plug adaptor for any appliances you take. Otherwise you can easily buy the equipment in supermarkets or electronic stores.

If you're buying any electric equipment for use in Britain, check that it can be switched to UK voltage.

Florida Time

Most of Florida (except for the northwest panhandle west of River Apalachicola) is on Eastern Standard Time, which is GMT plus six hours. East Coast USA is usually five hours behind Britain, but sometimes six hours because of choosing different dates to switch between summer and winter. America's Daylight Saving Time runs from May to October. So take care when adjusting your watch from late March and during September-October!

Taxes

Florida operates a 6.5% VAT which they call sales tax on everything except basic food items. On hotel rooms most resorts levy a 4% local tax in addition to the 6.5% sales tax.

Telephones

For local calls from a public pay-phone, just dial the 7-figure number. The charge is 25 cents and coin boxes accept quarters, dimes and nickels.

Florida splits into four telephone regions, with area codes 305, 407, 813 and 904.

For long distance, hit 1 followed by area code and the seven-figure phone number.

Many companies have an '800' prefix, which enables you to call free. To raise the operator, dial 0. For an international operator, 00.

For international calls, dial 011 + country code (Britain is 44) + area code (dropping Britain's initial zero) + telephone number. Calling from your hotel room will roughly double the regular cost.

Long distance call rates are lower after 5 p.m., and still lower after 11 p.m. and on weekends and public holidays. For 'reverse charge' ask for a 'collect call'.

Tipping

Depending on quality and friendliness of service, tip waiters, bartenders, cabbies, barbers and hairdressers around 15 per cent of the total bill. Baggage porters usually get 50 cents per bag, minimum $1. For helpful chambermaids, reckon a dollar or two per night if you're staying several days.

What to wear

The Florida dress code is casual, cool and comfortable during the day; sportswear in the evening, jeans and trainers quite acceptable. Some up-market restaurants require jacket and tie for evening dining. During winter months, pack a sweater for cool periods. Air conditioning can make you shiver when you come in from the outdoor summer heat; so have a light sweater or jacket to take the chill off the indoor climates. Take a fold-up brolly or plastic mac for those summer-afternoon downpours.

Traffic rules

Drive on the right, overtake on the left. Lane discipline is tight, so don't weave!

At a red traffic light, you can make a right turn after coming to a full stop, and yielding for pedestrians and cars. On a flashing red light, come to a full stop, and proceed with caution. On a flashing yellow light, slow down and proceed with caution.

The normal highway speed limit is 55 mph, strictly enforced, but 65 mph on expressways in open country. Along the Florida Keys, the limit is 45 with short overtaking zones at 55 mph. In built-up areas, the range is well signposted, between 20 and 40 mph, or even 15 mph in school zones.

Watch for yellow-painted school buses! Traffic in both directions must stop when a school bus is loading or unloading, except when the bus is halted on the other side of a dual carriageway.

Front-seat passengers must belt up. Children under age three must be strapped into an approved car seat, which can be provided by most car rental companies.

Always keep coins handy for toll highways. Unmanned toll booths require exact money, tossed into a receptacle as you crawl past.

Interstate highways have red, white and blue signs. The principal routes have 1- or 2-digit numbers. Even-numbered routes run east-west; odd-numbered run north-south.

Ring roads – called loop or belt ways in American – have 3-digit numbers, the first digit even. They circle or bypass cities.

Spur routes have 3-digit numbers, the first digit odd. They lead into cities.

If you break down on an expressway, park on right shoulder, raise the bonnet, tie a handkerchief to the car aerial or door handle, and wait for rescue. Night-time, use the hazard-blinker.

When parked on the street, the vehicle should point in the same direction as the traffic flow.

Your driving licence is recognized in USA. Don't forget to pack it!

Money matters

It's best to travel with US dollar traveller cheques, and to ask your bank or travel agent to supply a starter kit of US dollar bills. They come in identical-size notes – 1, 5, 10, 20, 50, 100 and 500. Because they all look alike, same shade of green, scrutinize the figures carefully, and keep them sorted. Look before you hand over! It's very easy to give a ten-dollar tip instead of a one.

Because of a flourishing counterfeit industry, some shops and restaurants are reluctant to accept banknotes higher than $20. They are much happier with well-known credit cards, particularly Visa, Access/Mastercard, American Express, Diners, EuroCard and Carte Blanche.

In case your credit card goes missing, be sure to keep all number details separately from your credit-card wallet, with phone numbers to report loss.

For currency exchange, banking hours are generally Mon-Fri 9-16 or 17 hrs, closed Sat and Sun. Some major stores, hotels and theme parks can oblige.

Liquor laws

The legal drinking age is 21. Each municipality has its own local laws on the sale of alcohol.

Emergency Phone

For fire, police or ambulance dial 911.

British Consulates

Miami – Brickell Bay Office Tower, 1001 S. Bayshore Drive, Suite 2110. Tel: 305/374-1522. Fax: 305/374-8196.

Public holidays

New Year's Day; 3rd Monday in Jan – Martin Luther King's Day; 3rd Monday in Feb – Presidents' Day; Good Friday; last Monday in May – Veterans Memorial Day; July 4 – Independence Day; first Monday in Sep – Labor Day; 2nd Monday in Oct – Columbus Day; 1st Tuesday after the 1st Monday of Nov in even-numbered years – General Election Day; Nov 11 – Veterans' Day; 4th Thursday in Nov – Thanksgiving Day; Christmas Day.

Senior Citizens

The numbers of retired folk living in Florida make up a formidable Senior Citizen lobby. For anyone over 60, or sometimes even 55, there are many entrance discounts to theme parks, museums, State parks etc. Numerous hotels and motels offer lower room rates, particularly outside the high season of Christmas to Easter. Restaurants feature Senior Citizen meals – not quite such enormous portions, but certainly at a lower price. Don't be shy of claiming your concession!

Florida's main attractions

Notes: Prices may change – usually upwards – but the figures should give reasonable guidance on cost subject to 6.5% State Tax. Senior citizens often qualify for reduced prices. Child prices are generally for ages 3 to 11 or 12, but that can vary greatly. Closing times are often extended during peak seasons.

ATTRACTION	CITY	HOURS	ADULT	CHILD
African Safari Park	Naples	9.30-17.30	$ 7.95	$ 5.95
Arabian Nights Dinner Show	Kissimmee	19.30	$30.00	$18.00
Bellm's Car & Music	Sarasota	8.30-18	$ 7.50	$ 3.75
Busch Gardens	Tampa	9.30-18	$29.75	Free under 3
Central Florida Zoo	Sanford	9-17	$ 5.00	$ 3.00
Church Street Station	Orlando	11-2am	$16.00	$10.00
Coral Castle	Homestead	9-21	$ 7.75	$ 4.50
Edison Winter Home	Ft. Myers	9-16	$ 7.00	$ 3.00
Elvis Presley Museum	Orlando	10-23	$ 4.00	$ 3.00
Everglades Wonder Garden	Bonita Springs	9-17	$ 5.00	$ 2.00
Fairchild Tropical Garden	Miami	9.30-16.30	$ 5.00	free
Florida Citrus Tower	Clermont	8-18	$ 1.75	$ 1.00
Florida Cypress Gardens	Cypress Gardens	9-18	$22.20	$15.30
Florida Silver Springs	Ocala	9-17	$21.15	$16.00
Florida Sunken Gardens	St. Petersburg	9-17.30	$ 5.25	$ 3.00
Florida Weeki Wachee	Weeki Wachee	9-18	$10.95	$ 6.95
Fred Bear Museum	Gainesville	10-17	$ 2.00	$ 1.00

ATTRACTION	CITY	HOURS	ADULT	CHILD
Ft. Liberty Dinner Show	Kissimmee	at 18.30 & 21	$30.00	$20.00
Fun World	Sanford	10-24		
Gatorland Zoo	Orlando	8-19	$10.55	$ 7.37
Green Meadows Farm	Kissimmee	9.30-15	$ 9.00	$ 9.00
H.M.S. Bounty	Miami	12-20	$ 3.50	$ 1.50
Homosassa Springs	Homosassa	9-17.30	$ 6.95	$ 3.95
Jungle Queens	Ft. Lauderdale	10-14	$ 7.00	$ 5.00
Key West City Tour Train	Key West	9-16	$ 9.00	$ 3.00
King Henry's Feast Dinner	Orlando	at 18.30 & 21	$30.00	$20.00
Leu Botanical Gardens	Orlando	9-17	$ 3.00	$ 1.00
Lightner Museum	St. Augustine	9-17	$ 3.00	$ 1.00
Lion Country Safari	W. Palm Beach	9.30-17.30	$11.95	$ 9.95
Luau Sea World Show	Orlando	at 18.35	$23.95	$16.95
Mardi Gras Dinner Show	Orlando	at 18.30 & 21	$30.00	$20.00
Marineland	St. Augustine	9-17.30	$ 9.95	$ 4.95
Medieval Times	Kissimmee	at 18 & 21	$28.00	$20.00
Miami Metro Zoo	Miami	10-17.30	$ 8.25	$ 4.25
Miami Museum of Science & Planetarium	Miami	10-18	$ 8.50	$ 5.00
Miami Seaquarium	Miami	9.30-18.30	$17.00	$12.00
Monkey Jungle	Miami	9.30-17	$ 7.50	$ 4.00
Mystery Fun House	Orlando	10-23	$ 6.95	
Ocean World	Ft. Lauderdale	10-18	$10.95	$ 8.95

ATTRACTION	CITY	HOURS	ADULT	CHILD
Orlando Science Center	Orlando	9-17	$ 4.00	$ 3.00
Potter Wax Museum	St. Augustine	9-17	$ 3.95	$ 2.25
Ringling Museum of Art	Sarasota	10-18	$ 5.00	$ 1.75
Rivership Romance	Sanford			
Salvador Dali Museum	St. Petersburg	10-17	$ 3.50	$ 2.50
Sea World of Florida	Orlando	9-22	$32.00	$28.00
Seascape	Pt. Canaveral & Miami		$99.00	$39.00
Spaceport USA	Pt. Canaveral	9-dusk	free	
bus tour			$ 7.00	$ 4.00
Astronaut Hall of Fame	Titusville	9-dusk	$ 7.00	$ 5.00
Universal Studios	Orlando	9-23		
One-day			$35.00	$27.56
Two-day			$56.18	$44.52
Water Mania	Kissimmee	10-17	$18.00	$16.00
Wet 'n' Wild	Orlando	10-18	$20.00	$18.00
Walt Disney World Resort:	Orlando	9-20		
One-day One Theme Park Passport			$35.90	$28.50
Four-day Three Parks Passport			$124.60	$97.15
Five-day Super Pass			$171.15	$135.20
Walt Disney World River Country		10-17	$13.25	$10.60
River Country/Discovery Island combined			$16.70	$12.19
Walt Disney World Pleasure Island			$12.65	$12.65
Walt Disney World Typhoon Lagoon			$20.67	$16.43